Mind Power
for children

JOHN KEHOE
NANCY FISCHER

Zoetic Inc.
P.O. Box 48823
595 Burrard Street, Bentall Centre
Vancouver, British Columbia, Canada V7X 1A6

www.learnmindpower.com

First edition
Canadian Cataloguing in Publication Data
Kehoe, John
Mind Power for Children: the guide for parents
and teachers

ISBN 0-9697551-7-1

1. Child rearing.
2. Cognition in children.
3. Success in children.
4. Self-actualization
   (Psychology) in children.

I. Fischer, Nancy, 1953- II. Title.

BF723.S77K43 2002
 649'.1   C2001-903374-5

We gratefully acknowledge permission to reprint
an excerpt from Harry Potter and the Prisoner of
Azkaban Copyright © J.K. Rowling 1999

Illustrations by Brad Turk

Printed and bound in Canada
by Transcontinental Printing

MIND POWER

mindpower

FOR
CHILDREN

contents

ACKNOWLEDGEMENTS

*Every book is a distinct experience that has many
unseen hands contributing to its inevitable unfolding.*

*We would like to thank Carla Heslop, Sharyn
Devereux Blum and Paul Blum for their input,
suggestions, stories and consultation. Thanks are also
due to Brad Turk for his illustrations, to Cher Bloom for
her photography, and to Jim Emerson for his
innovative page layouts, as well as the front and back
cover. To Ric and Jennifer Beairsto for their editing and
guidance of the project through to fruition, to our
families for their constant support, and finally to the
thousands of parents, teachers and children who have
contributed and supplied us with inspiration
throughout the years, thank you all.*

mindpower

i

FOR

CHILDREN

Introduction

As a teacher, I have devoted almost thirty years of my life to researching, lecturing and writing about the powers of the mind. In 1987 I wrote the book *Mind Power*, which went on to become a number one international bestseller, selling over a million copies. Ten years later, it was updated and re-released as *Mind Power Into the 21st Century.*

Writing a bestseller is a unique experience, and I heartily recommend it to everyone. Not only is it career enhancing and gratifying both financially and emotionally, but it allows one to reach a large audience, and it was this aspect I found most exciting. Through innumerable radio, TV and newspaper interviews, I have had the rare opportunity to share my insights and passion about the human potential. The key to unlocking the genius that exists within each of us, I have discovered, is to harness and utilize the powers of the human mind.

In the early years of my teaching, my emphasis was on instructing adults, but it soon became apparent that another segment of our society could benefit from these practices. Parents and teachers would regularly ask me, "How can we teach mind power to children?"

While it seemed obvious that teaching children mind power practices early in their education would offer them a discernible advantage, how to design and teach such a program remained the challenge. Here synchronicity played a crucial role, as it so often does, in attracting the necessary people to champion such an endeavor. Over the following several years, I met three groups of educators, who, independently of one another, and using the methods and techniques drawn from my *Mind Power* book, had decided to teach young children mind power. Carla Heslop and Claire McCormick had founded the Positive Start program; Sharyn Devereux Blum and her husband Paul Blum had created their New Horizons course to assist young children and teenagers, and Nancy Fischer; my co-author on this book, had been instrumental in designing the Mind Power for Children program. Working closely with these talented and dedicated individuals, the first Mind Power for Children program was presented, and was an immediate success.

Through facilitating these programs, we discovered that self-esteem, courage, and positive qualities of character need not be left to chance in children, but can be encouraged and imprinted using mind power techniques. We further concluded that we can all parent and teach more effectively using these methods. These

iii

mindpower

simple yet revolutionary techniques can and should be taught at a very early age, and when applied regularly, will significantly enhance a child's development in a very positive way.

My co-writer Nancy Fischer has been an early childhood and primary school teacher for twenty years, is a parent of two daughters and an innovative and well-respected educator. Her dedication and commitment to this project, and her uncanny ability to bring out the best in children, is one of the reasons why the Mind Power for Children program has been so successful.

This book has been a labor of love, and is the culmination of many years experience. The stories contained herein are drawn from the experiences of children, parents and teachers who have followed the mind power system. There was no problem finding these success stories; the challenge was to choose from the multitude that presented themselves to us over the years.

The program we share in these pages is one that has now been taught for more than ten years to thousands of children worldwide. Our purpose in writing this book is to share our experience, and to change the world one child at a time. If this book can assist in that goal, then we have done a great work.

John Kehoe

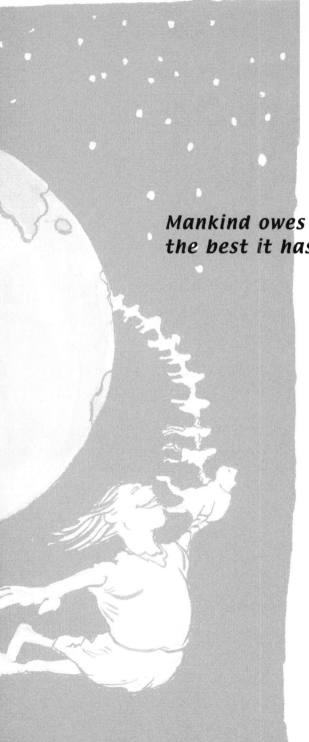

Mankind owes to the child the best it has to give...

THE OPENING
WORDS TO THE
UNITED NATIONS'
DECLARATION OF
THE RIGHTS OF
THE CHILD

1

TEACHING MIND POWER

Teaching Mind Power

Thoughts are the most powerful forces in a child's universe. The thoughts children think each day influence every aspect of their lives. Their attitudes, choices, personality, and who they ultimately become as individuals, are all products of their thinking.

We all want our children to have positive attitudes, make wise choices and feel good about themselves. This is obvious. What is not so obvious is how to achieve this. Courses in thinking have never been part of the regular school curriculum. How to think with purpose and clarity is a skill that needs to be taught at home. It falls upon us as parents to instill good thinking habits in our children.

Until recently, little was known or understood about the science of mind power. Fortunately this is no longer true. Now, at the beginning of the 21st century, mind power is a well-respected practice used daily by millions. Contemporary media, whether it be mass circulation magazines, TV documentaries or scholarly publications such as *The New England Journal of Medicine*, abound in material extolling the virtues of training the mind. Sports icons such as Tiger Woods and Michael Jordan share how mental training complements their physical workouts, with noticeable results. Entertainment celebrities like Arnold Schwarzenegger and Jim Carrey speak glowingly of the results they've achieved by using mind power. It has become almost common knowledge that mind power techniques such as visualization and affirmations, practiced regularly, increase performance.

However, even with all this attention, the practice of mind power has been overlooked by perhaps the most influential segment of our society – parents. For whatever reason, it seems to have eluded parents and teachers that what has worked so successfully with adults could be adapted and taught to children. Everyone assumed that mind power was an adult practice, that young children would be unable to understand or use these methods. Fortunately, this is not the case. Children not only take easily to mind power, but thrive using the techniques.

MY THOUGHTS ARE REAL FORCES!

We have spent the last ten years teaching the unique Mind Power program presented in this book to thousands of children of all ages. The results have been spectacular and lasting. Children's potential was explored and expanded in ways we had not even envisioned when we began our first program. Their stories fill this book. Our hope is that by sharing these experiences, you will feel inspired to follow this path with the children in your life.

Understanding Thoughts As Energy

Mind power is based upon the scientific discovery that everything at its purest and deepest essence is energy. The walls in your home, the clothes you are wearing, the book in your hands, all are at the most basic level vibrating energy. Our thoughts too consist of this same energy, and are powerful forces in and of themselves. Thought is forever attempting to find form, is always looking for an outlet, always trying to manifest itself into its physical equivalent.

Our thoughts can be compared to sparks from a fire. Though they contain the essence and potential power of the flame, they manifest as a flash and then dissipate quickly. They last only a few seconds. Because of this, a single unaided thought may not seem to have much power in and of itself. However, through repetition, our thoughts can become concentrated and directed, and their force is magnified many times. The more a thought is repeated, the more energy and power it generates, resonating within us and attracting from the outer reality the circumstances that match the images we hold within. Our experiences in life, and the thoughts we think, are directly related to one another. Understanding this, we encourage our children to work creatively with their thoughts in a fun and systematic way.

The habits we form from childhood make no small difference, but rather they make all the difference.
» Aristotle

Educators and child psychologists have long known that self-esteem, self-image and personality characteristics are formed early in a child's development. What has not been fully appreciated is how dramatically mind power practices, taught early, can encourage positive qualities in a child's life, enhancing their ability to function in their environment with confidence and assurance.

Keeping It Simple

Teaching mind power to children is much like teaching any other subject. Know your material and present it clearly and enthusiastically. Above all, be patient. Trying to squeeze in a quick lesson on mind power as you run out the door on the way to work could very possibly result in a negative rather than a positive experience. Allowing time and space for these "lessons" will keep the techniques *fun* – probably the most effective element in teaching anything to children, especially young ones.

There are four main techniques used in our program: affirmations, visualization, acknowledging and eliminating negatives. Through practicing these techniques, children come to realize and experience the power of their thoughts. Each technique is explored fully in the following chapters.

Recognizing the "Teachable Moments"

The mind power techniques described in this book can be taught even in the earliest years. In order to be most effective, watch for and identify what educators call "teachable moments." Teachable moments are those times when your child is most attentive, ready to listen and ripe for the next step, guidance, or bit of information that will spark some insight or action.

You've undoubtedly noticed how children's biological clocks are different from adults. Any parent who has been wakened by a lively

four-year-old at 6 A.M., knows only too well they can be bundles of energy at that hour, raring to go. Many preschoolers are very alert and eager for stimulation when they first wake up in the morning. If they're dragging their heels in getting

> *The best teaching moments aren't ones that are planned.*
> » Michele Borba

dressed for school, it likely has more to do with the distractions around them (and preoccupation with their own thoughts) than sleepiness. Talking about dreams over breakfast can be a spring-board for introducing visualizations. Plans for the day can lead to discussing affirmations. Before bed or an afternoon quiet time pre-sent excellent opportunities to use acknowledgements, especially since many school-aged children will naturally choose this time to "download" their day and perhaps even share their fears or worries with you.

Teachable moments can pop up when you least expect it – during a car ride or waiting in a bank lineup. Observe your child's "receptive" times, as they can be valuable educational opportunities.

Persistence

Your children may have to practice a technique several times before they fully grasp how it works or begin seeing results. Other times positive changes will take place almost immediately, which is always thrilling. More often, however, it will take a few days or even a week or more of using the techniques before either of you discern a noticeable difference. Because the exercises are fun and enjoyable, children are usually more than willing to continue practicing until results are achieved. Eventually, with a few successes under her belt, even the most tentative child will begin to feel more confident.

Mind power is a practice, not simply a momentary change in attitude. In this skill, as in most others, repetition is the key to success. You don't learn to play a piano in only one or two lessons; so too with mind power. Our role as parents, teachers or caregivers is to gently encourage our children to do their exercises. As diligent as we are at reminding them to brush their teeth, the same attention is required to keep children using mind power, especially in the beginning, before the techniques have become a natural part of their thinking.

"Did you do your affirmations today, Lisa?"
"No, I forgot."
"Well, let's do them right now. It'll only take a minute.
Come on, we'll say them together, sweetheart."

Children are usually eager to try something new, and, with your support and enthusiasm, will readily experiment with the techniques. Positive re-enforcement certainly helps as well.

"I noticed how quickly you were able to finish your homework

tonight, Josh. Your affirmations are really working for you!"

Like all of us, children thrive on encouragement. Any evidence of success, even just remembering to *do* the practices, is a reason to celebrate and acknowledge your child's effort. If we keep our comments honest and sincere, our children will feel supported and empowered. Remember, we may be the coach but it is still our child's game. The goal is to have our children recognize the power of their own thoughts. Once this is established, a new way of thinking will become second nature to them, and they will have learned skills that will carry them through a lifetime of challenges.

The Power of Words

Our choice of words helps to direct our child's thoughts. Words paint a picture in a child's mind that he will tend to act upon. Just as behavior is a kinesthetic expression of our thoughts and feelings (and a lot of parents' time and energy is spent managing children's behavior), so too are words a verbal expression of our thoughts and feelings. A good rule to remember is: the last words your child hears create images in his mind, and that is what he will act upon. The images that the words evoke are more important than the words themselves. A lot of mixed messages are sent when our verbal instructions don't accurately reflect the behavior we are seeking from our children.

"Be careful what you ask for... you might get it."

mindpower

Recently, at a community center, a child near me began running down the length of the swimming pool. It looked as if he was carrying a message from his mother to siblings at the far end of the pool. "Don't run," called his mother. The child stopped for a moment and then, his mission foremost in his mind, he took off again at high speed. "I said, "Don't run!" shouted his mother. He stopped, for a few seconds this time, reflecting on what she had said, and then took off again, running even faster. "Won't that child ever learn?" his mother grumbled. Yes, her child *will* learn, but it will happen more quickly if he were told *what* to do instead of what *not* to do. If she had called "walk," or even, "Ben, please walk," she would have been much more likely to have evoked the response she wanted. (Calling your child's name first gets their immediate attention.)

Our children need correct behavioral information to act appropriately, because whatever information they receive, they are bound to act upon. Here is another example of how our choice of words can elicit the opposite behavior of what we intend.

Our school recently installed a new slide in the children's playground, and the parents who had worked hard to raise the funds for the slide were understandably very proud of it. It was also expensive, so we wanted it looked after.

You can imagine my surprise when I arrived at school one morning and my daughter's teacher said to me in despair, "Look at how the children are behaving on our new slide. You'd never know that I keep going over those rules with the children, day after day, would you?" She then showed me the rules. They were written in huge letters on a large blackboard for all to see:

> *No fighting on the slide.*
> *No sliding on your stomach.*
> *No climbing up the slide.*
> *No throwing gravel down the slide.*

I looked out the window again. One child was climbing up the slide as another threw gravel down it. My daughter's teacher was unintentionally focusing the children's thoughts on behavior she did not want, and that is exactly what she was getting.

Another school, not far away, took the exact opposite approach by letting the children know what positive actions they expected from them. In the hall was a giant poster stating:

> *In our school we...*
> *Walk in the hall.*
> *Share.*

Work quietly.

Play cooperatively.

They were giving the children very clear and concise directions and, not surprisingly, the children followed them beautifully.

The phrases we use when we speak to our children are important because certain words trigger particular responses. For example, "*Please speak quietly,*" is a clear and positive request. "*Don't shout,*" tells children that shouting is unacceptable, but does not

teach them what to replace the unacceptable behavior with. Moreover, "shout" becomes the visual image in the child's mind. Consequently they may well continue to shout, even though they know it is not appropriate, simply because that is the only behavioral instruction they have received.

Understanding the nature of our child's mind allows us to teach them in more effective ways. It also becomes self-evident that any method that helps to direct their thoughts towards positive outcomes is a valuable tool in parenting.

Mind Power for Children

Mind power is a great gift to us parents and teachers. It makes our job easier and gives us specific tools to work with. It is also a wonderful blessing for our children, because it gives them a discernible advantage in life. Mind power children are happier and more successful than other children. They have self-confidence, perform well at school and make friends easily. Positive children get sick less often and are more creative and adventurous. Sure, they have their moods and difficulties, the same as other children, but results indicate that they rebound more quickly from these setbacks and have an uncanny knack of coming out ahead. This is what every parent desires with all their heart for their children. Little did we suspect that the key to our children's success and happiness lay in their minds, minds that are specifically designed to thrive when nourished with positive input.

Throughout all stages of childhood, there are numerous windows of opportunity for us to instill in our children high self-esteem and positive attitudes, to help them appreciate and know deeply not only their own uniqueness, but the uniqueness and wonder of life itself. As they grow and develop, our children can be praised, loved, and encouraged every step of the way. Mind power gives us these tools. In providing this support for our children, we do the greatest of all works: the parenting of the magical child into a self-actualized and self-fulfilled adult. What greater purpose could destiny possibly give us?

Tips
for Teaching Mind Power

1 Try to keep the lessons fun and light-hearted. Regular repetition of the techniques is the key to successful results. However, some children may build up resistance if they feel pressured to treat the exercises as "work" rather than "play." Pick times that feel appropriate, and again, the key is *fun*.

2 Practice positive speech habits. You may have to relearn some of the ways you give directions or ask for a particular kind of behavior by paying special attention to the words you use. Remember, "Sweetheart, walk across the street," suggests to the child that she walk, while, "Don't run across the street," is a signal to run, because running is the last instruction she heard and therefore is the image she will retain.

mindPower

3

MIND POWER

Encourage your child to believe that anything is possible. You will be amazed by what can happen when you teach the mind power techniques to your children, and in turn apply them to your own life. Each generation forges beyond the one preceding it, whether it's by inventing the cure for an illness or growing the most delicious carrots in the world. Your child's potential and place in this world is unlimited and vital.

4

Study mind power techniques yourself. If you haven't already joined the more than one million readers of *Mind Power Into the 21st Century*, then we highly recommend that you use it as a companion resource to this book. The most effective way to teach our children mind power is to model it ourselves. Our children are biologically geared to take reality clues from us. They are willing to entertain and emulate any idea or concept that we ourselves practice and believe. Let's give the "little copycats" lots of positive examples to follow.

2

CONSCIOUS PARENTING

Conscious Parenting

Conscious parenting, from a mind power perspective, is making daily child-rearing decisions with the awareness that who we are is equally as important as how we interact with our children. Both aspects play a crucial role in children's development. Conscious parenting means understanding ourselves and looking within to discover the underlying reasons behind why we act and feel the way we do. As conscious parents we strive to ensure that our parenting practices accurately model the positive example we want our children to emulate.

It is not always easy. It takes vision and commitment, and often we make mistakes, leaving us feeling frustrated. The truth is, being a parent is one of life's great reminders that we are indeed human, and bound to make many mistakes along the way. Learning from our mistakes and moving on is the key. We do this in a conscious and loving way, respecting both our children and ourselves.

Personal Archeology

"I shouted at my eight-year-old son to pick up his toys, told him not to be so lazy and irresponsible. I momentarily lost it as I berated him unmercifully. Then, as I slammed the door shut to his room for effect, I realized, with horror, that this was exactly what my father used to do to me. Yelling and belittlement.

I had become my father." » Doug

How often do we hear our parent's voice echoing in the distance as we interact with our children? Like it or not, we are the product of our upbringing, and the models of parenting we instinctively use are those of our parents. Most likely, in many situations, our "gut" reaction will be to repeat the exact same methods that we ourselves experienced as children. Or in other cases, we might be so determined to reject our parents' ways that we tend to overcompensate.

"I never had anything as a child so now I try to give my son everything. I know I shouldn't and maybe I'm spoiling him, but I can't help it. I keep remembering how deprived I felt." » Angela

Whether we model our parents' methodology closely or overcompensate by doing the opposite, the fact remains, how we were parented has a huge influence on how we, in turn, parent. It happens naturally and mostly unconsciously. We find ourselves reacting impulsively in the heat of the moment, often without realizing what we've said or done until it's over.

In speaking to groups on parenting, we explore the area of personal archeology by looking at our own upbringing. The following questions are often starting points from which we can examine our own private and unique mythology.

mindpower

22

1. When you were growing up, were you treated as though you were special, with qualities that were unique to you?
2. Were you told that you could do and be anything you wanted to, and that you'd be loved and admired no matter what it was you chose?
3. What happened if things didn't go exactly as you had hoped? Did your parents suggest positive solutions, or advise you to quit?
4. Did the adults around you seem happy with their lives? Were they models of success and contentment who were genuinely pleased when you were successful as well?

Regardless of whether we answer "yes" or "no" to these questions, our challenge is to examine why the adults around us may have acted the way they did. What effect did their actions have on us as children, and how might we either adopt or alter their ways when dealing with our *own* children. These questions always provoke a lively discussion that is quite revealing.

"My parents always encouraged me to go for what I wanted in life and said that whatever I chose was okay with them ... as long as when I was finished I joined the family hardware business." ›› Jean

"I have many fond memories of my dad helping me with my math homework Sunday nights. What an amazingly patient guy he was. Now I hope I can be the same way with my own children." ›› Greg

Personal archeology involves looking closely at our past and asking ourselves questions: How am I like my parents? How am I different? What negative or positive patterns am I repeating? Through this process we can identify from our own upbringing what was constructive, nurturing and supportive, and emulate these techniques in our relationship with our children.

Similarly we can also identify and "let go" of patterns and beliefs that are outmoded, unproductive, or hurtful. Our intention at all times is to gain understanding and wisdom, not to dredge up sadness or anger that will only serve to cloud our vision. Be generous and remember, our parents were human too. Mind power gives us the tools that our parents never had. It allows us to understand ourselves and helps us to make constructive changes.

Being a Positive Model

Our thoughts and beliefs, combined with our habitual actions, are what we daily pass on to our children. We are the model they look up to. This can be both beneficial and detrimental. It's valuable when we are modeling behavior we wish them to imitate, but sometimes, even with the best intentions, we send children the wrong message. For example, in times when we are feeling anxious and overprotective, we may inadvertently be teaching our children to fear unknown situations, rather than embrace them. Other times, when we find ourselves feeling very upbeat and ready to conquer the world, we in turn pass this courageous attitude on to our children. Let's face it, all of us have both our "on" and "off" days. Nobody's perfect and we needn't expect ourselves to be. We must, however, be aware that through our actions we are constantly modeling examples for our children to follow.

"The other afternoon, as my daughter and I walked home from preschool, we passed a young woman sitting on a blanket asking for spare change. She was unkempt and looked like she really hadn't eaten properly for quite some time, so instinctively I put some change in her cup. As I did, I remembered how my parents had always taught us to treat others with dignity. Once my mother even took me with her as she delivered sandwiches to people on the street who looked a lot like this young woman.

As we walked on, I told my daughter the story about my mother's kindness. My daughter then asked

if we too could give some food to the homeless people we saw. It made me realize what a powerful impression our actions make on our children. Not only had my mother taught me to care for those less fortunate, but now this positive value was being passed on to a new generation through me." » Maya

Who we are is the key to what our children will become.

"Thank God, children grow up one day at a time. Otherwise I'd be a basket-case worrying about every little mistake I make along the way." » Thomas, parent of two

If we want our children to have patience, we need to demonstrate, through example, patience in our life, not once in a while but regularly and consistently. If we want them to make friends, then let us have lots of friends ourselves. If we want them to be considerate and caring for others, then we must model consideration and care. Gandhi said, "We must be the change that we want to see in the world." So too we must demonstrate how we want our children to be in the world. There's no other way. 'Do what I say and not what I do,' simply doesn't work.

"I watched my seven-year-old son really nagging at his three-year-old sister for walking so slowly as we returned home from the park. He was eager to get back for a favorite television show

*and was relentlessly teasing her. I began to admonish him for his impatience when I remembered clearly an incident a day earlier when I had been equally impatient in calling on him to dress faster for school. It suddenly dawned on me that I've been impatient almost all of my life. I also realized that if I expect my children to follow my good example, I'm going to have to change. That was several months ago, and I'm happy to say that I'm learning to be more patient and allow more time for things, like getting my children ready for school. I'm feeling much less stressed and, not surprisingly, I'm starting to see changes in my son as well. Actions **do** speak louder than words."* ›› Chizu

> *Children have never been very good at listening to their elders, but they have never failed to imitate them.*
> ›› James Baldwin

Through understanding ourselves, and noticing what we are modeling for our children, we can choose, if necessary, to make adjustments in our behavior.

Ultimately we must look closely at ourselves, without being overly harsh or exaggerating either our strengths or weaknesses, to see what we're reflecting for our children. It is ironic that while we often will not make changes to improve our own lives, we will do it for our children. This is another of the gifts children give us – they call upon us to be the very best we can be.

> *I was a wonderful parent before I had children.*
> *I was an expert on why everyone was having*
> *problems with theirs. Then I had three of my own.*
>
> » Adele Faber and Elaine Mazlish

Let's Take a Chance and Raise Their Hopes

A common fear that has crept into many parents' consciousness is that of raising their children's hopes "unrealistically." What's more, in their attempts to not raise their children's hopes unrealistically, some parents have inadvertently gone one step further and have become afraid to raise their hopes at all.

Why is there this terrible fear that one day a child will "hope too much?" What is "too much" anyway? Is it such a terrible thing that

our child decides to strive for some goal that we or the neighbors think is unattainable. Who is it to say what exactly is unattainable and what isn't? Where would the world be today if every outrageous idea and dream had been dismissed or squashed at its inception?

Why not let our children be as hopeful as they like. If we've done our job properly they will either achieve their fantastic goals, or they won't and they will cope. Children naturally dare to hope and aim for things that are even greater than we can imagine for them. They may not obtain them all, but they may well achieve many.

OLYMPICS HERE I COME!

The young do not know enough to be prudent; and therefore, they attempt the impossible - and achieve it, generation after generation.

» Pearl S. Buck

Let's bring children up to believe that dreams do come true, that often you can achieve the impossible, that you can have what you want in life if you're willing to work for it. If we tell our children that there is always a way, then, if at first they don't succeed, they will keep looking and eventually find it.

Instead of fearing that by using mind power techniques, our children's hopes may be raised only to be dashed, let us be brave enough to allow our children to define their own standards of success, and recognize that their vision may extend far beyond our own.

Living in the Cyber Age

It's certainly true that contemporary culture and media bombard our children with many contradictory messages and values, many of them quite unsavory, others just limiting. Music, books, magazines, movies, TV, the Internet, and countless other influences have their effect, both positive and negative. But even with all this input they receive, it is indisputable that we, as parents, are the primary and most important role models. If we can get this right, we can go a long way toward helping our children be aware and responsible.

Talk with your children about values and notions of right and wrong. What does it mean to be a conscious citizen? How can we help the world and each other? Too lofty a subject for a five-year-old? You'd be surprised. Even the youngest child can contribute ideas about helping and getting along with others and doing good in the world. Teach your children to respect all human beings and to appreciate their differences. Help them to see that we are all important parts of the great mosaic that makes up the human race.

With the advances of modern technology, our children are now exposed to a range of opinions, images and ideas far beyond what we ourselves experienced, and this is happening at a younger and younger age. We need not fear this bombardment if we teach our children well. As

> *The greatest gifts my parents gave to me . . . were their unconditional love and a set of values. Values that they lived and didn't just lecture about.*
> ›› Colin Powell

parents we can still transmit traditional values of honesty, fairness, and respect for self and others. Model and encourage what you hold important, through both word and deed. Your children will naturally follow your example even if there are some detours along the way.

Tips
for Being a Conscious Parent

1 Take some time to ask yourself, "Are any of my present habits or beliefs holding me back from being the best parent I can be?"

2 Make a list of the attributes you would like to see in your children, and beside these attributes note what you are presently modeling for them. Any discrepancies? Remember, children are wide open to suggestion by example. Their capabilities are still forming. They are ready to believe or become anything, so why not give them the very best example you can.

F O R

C H I L D R E N

3 Look for ways to illustrate to your children how you find happiness and fulfillment in your own life. Share your feelings of success around the dinner table, whether it's through your job, your hobbies, your home, or friends and family. What children recognize is how empowered and happy we *appear* in our lives. It isn't the occupation we have, the position we hold, or the amount of money we make that impresses our children. It's the expression of happiness, success, and contentment that we model for our children that makes an impact.

4 Take a close look at the other models in your child's life. If there is a certain characteristic you would like your child to possess, and a good friend possesses it in abundance, this person can be a mentor to your child. Seek out opportunities to introduce your child to positive role models in your family and community.

3
AFFIRMATIONS

Affirmations

Like a computer, our mind processes all the information we input. Our beliefs and expectations are built up by the thoughts and suggestions we regularly give ourselves. So too with children. Our child's mind is incredibly active with thousands of thoughts each day. Affirmations – short simple statements that we repeat to ourselves either internally or out loud – can effectively direct those thoughts towards a particular purpose.

For very young children, parents and caregivers can speak affirmations directly to their children, helping to both build their vocabulary and empower them. Young children love to hear positive statements about their worth and abilities, especially spoken aloud by people whom they love and respect. As children grow and their language develops, they will learn to use affirmations themselves to direct their minds towards picturing desirable outcomes.

For example, if your child is worried about an upcoming test, you could teach him to repeat to himself, "I'm going to do really well... I'm going to do really well... I'm going to do really well." By reciting this positive statement over and over again for several minutes, the mind, like a horse being led to water, is led to consider "doing well." The mind shifts from the worry, to confidence (or whatever the affirmation is suggesting). Affirmations also affect actions. As a result of the positive stimulus his mind is feeding him, he may even study an extra half hour before going to bed. Most importantly, he'll start *thinking* about "doing well," and expecting the best in his performance.

When children feel depressed, worried, or fearful, as everyone occasionally does, it is usually because of the thoughts they're thinking. Negative thoughts like, "Nobody likes me," or "I'm going to fail the exam," almost always come to children as auditory messages, as opposed to a mental picture. It's like a little annoying voice inside them saying, "I'm going to fail," or, "Nobody likes me."

We can help our children overcome their doubts and fears by *also* using the power of words, but in a constructive way. The key is to show them how they can change the negative words inside their heads into positive verbal suggestions. That's exactly what affirmations do.

" 'The incantation is this –' Lupin cleared his throat, '*expecto patronum!*'
'Expecto patronum,' Harry repeated under his breath, 'expecto patronum.'
'Concentrating hard on your happy memory?'
'Oh – yeah –' said Harry, quickly forcing his thoughts back to that first broom-ride. 'Expecto patrono – no, patronum – sorry – expecto patronum, expecto patronum –'
Something whooshed suddenly out of the end of his wand; it looked like a wisp of silvery gas.
'Did you see that?' said Harry excitedly. 'Something happened!' "
»   J. K. Rowling
- excerpt from *Harry Potter and the Prisoner of Azkaban*

The recent Harry Potter phenomenon has done wonders to reintroduce the element of magic into modern children's literature. It's actually no surprise that Ms. Rowling's readership has spanned all generations. Humanity has always been in awe of supernatural powers. Magical incantations such as "abracadabra" have been used throughout the ages in hundreds of mythical tales by magicians and sorcerers who, with that one word, could cause astonishing mira-

38

mindpower

cles to take place. Children have long been fascinated by the magic power of words. Affirmations can have the same miraculous effect on how children feel and perceive their world. What makes mind power so extraordinary is that when children use affirmations, they are accessing the magical power of their *own minds.*

An easy way to describe to your child the power of affirmations is to compare the mind to a tape recorder. It's always on, recording each one of our thoughts. Whatever thought we think, whether it's happy or sad, positive or negative, it is recorded. For example, when we find ourselves in a situation that reminds us of a past negative experience, our mind plays back for us one of the old thought tapes. While we can't change the unpleasant experiences that have already taken place, we can change how we react to similar situations. By encouraging our mind to picture positive expectations through the use of affirmations, we eventually record over the negative thought tapes with new positive thoughts. Your child will be thrilled to

I CAN DO ANYTHING I PUT MY MIND TO.

know that he has the power to change his own thoughts simply with words, and you can encourage him to try it in numerous situations.

My son, Greg, age seven, was feeling particularly negative one morning – didn't like this, didn't like that: school, people, the world, himself. I quietly suggested that maybe things could improve if he changed his attitude, his thinking. I was pleased to catch a moment when he was receptive to a new idea, and he asked how he could change his thinking. I reminded him about affirmations, suggesting he choose something he wanted to improve.

*Greg sat quietly for a minute or two and then blurted out, "I'm never gonna be the last one finished my printing again!" Greg's teacher had told me earlier that he often had trouble completing his work before the recess break, and it seemed he was getting pretty frustrated. I reminded Greg that although I understood he wanted to complete his work faster, affirmations need to state what you **want** to have happen, not what you **don't** want.*

"Make it into a positive statement," I suggested. "How about, 'I can finish my work on time.' Is that what you want to happen?" "Yeah," he said, "so I don't miss any recess!" After a few more refinements, Greg came up with, "I can finish my work before recess." Again he sat quietly and really worked at absorbing this

new message. I was pleased he was attempting something with a positive attitude, but I did caution him that it could take a while for affirmations to work.

> **We are all works in progress, parents included.**
>
> ›› Elisa Medhus

The next day I was helping with reading in Greg's classroom. After reading was printing. Between the two subjects I went to the office to get something. When I came back Greg's teacher said to me, "He's usually the slowest to get going and to finish his printing, but today Greg got straight to it and was finished well before recess time." Naturally, she thought it was because I was in the classroom that morning, but I had actually been in the classroom helping once a week for the whole year. Greg and I looked at one another. I hadn't thought his affirmation would come true in only one day!

The best news of all was that it stuck. Almost every day Greg was finished his printing in plenty of time before recess, and his whole demeanor around schoolwork changed to be more positive. Funny enough, the next time Greg heard me complain about something, he suggested that I use affirmations too. And he was right!
›› Jessica, a Mind Power parent

A bonus benefit of affirmations is that the very act of repeating these uplifting words brings about happy and positive feelings. Children start to feel better just by saying them. Affirmations can be used in almost any situation, and often with the most remarkable results.

Carla Heslop, co-founder of the Positive Start program, shares how she used affirmations to dramatically improve her daughter's reading ability.

My daughter, Eloise, was having difficulty reading. To help her along, I spent time teaching her to sound out words, bought her easy-to-read books to build up her confidence, and encouraged her to practice. As time went on I found that instead of improving, her reading got worse. She became more and more reluctant, and reading sessions at home turned quickly into emotional scenes. I soon realized that what I was doing with all my good intentions was reinforcing the unspoken message that she really was a poor reader (after all, children who are good at reading don't have to practice, practice, practice, or read the easy books). I was at a loss as to what to do.

I finally asked myself what was the outcome I desired for my daughter. I wanted her to be a really good reader. I decided on two steps of action to accomplish this.

First, I would act as if she were already a really good reader (and try to rebuild some of the confidence I had unwittingly destroyed).

42

mindpower

Secondly, I would use an affirmation to help create a new belief system in her and myself. The affirmation was, "Eloise, you're a really good reader."

Here's what happened. Later that day when Eloise arrived home from school I asked her if she had reading homework. She mumbled an unenthusiastic, "Yes."

"Great," I said, "I like hearing you read. You're a really good reader." She looked mighty surprised, as this was a change from my usual approach, but said nothing. Later, during our reading time I was determined to make no comments other than affirming ones. I let her read without hurrying her; I told her any words she didn't know without making her sound them out, and at the end of the grueling twenty minutes, I said, "Well done, Eloise. You're a really good reader." I put a tick in her reading homework book and wrote, "Well done," which I showed her. "Tell the teacher I wrote that," I said. I could tell Eloise was already feeling pleased and more confident.

I sent her off to school with another reminder to show her teacher my comment because she, Eloise, was a really good reader. I did the same thing that evening. There was a noticeable improvement in her reading (I still had to bite my lip at times so as not to correct her), but I was able to say truthfully at

the end, "You have improved, Eloise. You're a really good read-
er." Again I wrote, "Eloise is a really good reader" in her home-
work notebook. "Show the teacher," I said. Her little face was
glowing.

The next day she came home from school singing, "I'm a really
good reader." She'd made up a song about it. Reading that night
was almost a pleasure for me. Eloise surprised me with some of
the multisyllable words she could read. Her speed also improved,
not to mention our relationship. It was amazing, and I was so
relieved. Every day after that I used the affirmation (without over-
doing it), and she even made her own sign (an affirmation card)
that we put up on the wall. Now, several years later, she has
become ... you guessed it – "a really good reader."

Poster Power

My daughter, Leah, was feeling like she didn't have many
friends. So I put "Leah has lots of friends" on a poster on her
bedroom mirror and encouraged her to say, "I have lots of
friends." A few days later Leah started talking of friends she was
making both outside and within her school environment. Friend-
ships seemed to blossom out of nowhere. Both she and I were
thrilled that the affirmations worked so well. ›› Chandra.

Affirmations are not just to be said; they can also be written on posters or big signs and put up on the wall. Start now! Get out the colored pens and cards and go crazy. You can also mount a chalk or white board in your child's room and on it write the day's affirmation. There are dozens of ways you can make affirmations a part of your child's life. Put them on a T-shirt, or make up songs with affirmations as lyrics. After all, isn't this exactly how many advertisements become imprinted in our minds? Say affirmations aloud while jumping up and down; create a snakes and ladders game with positive affirmations as ladders and negative thoughts as snakes. The possibilities are endless!

Printed affirmations can help as valuable reminders, often when we need it the most.

*Sarah asked me what to do about another child who was calling her names and saying she was "stupid" and "spoilt." She was really upset about the situation. We talked about different things she could do. Then she looked at her card on the wall that said, "**Sarah is special.**" She turned to me and said, "At least **we** know I'm special!"*

I asked Sarah a couple of weeks later how things were going with the other child. She looked at me blankly and asked, "What about him?" Then she carried on with what she was doing. It showed me that once she had resolved things for herself, the "situation" disappeared. ›› Kent

Some affirmations for you and your child to work with are:

I have lots of friends.	I'm full of good ideas.
I am a good friend to myself.	My imagination is fabulous.
I play well with others.	I have a wonderful mind.
I'm a good sport.	I am very creative.
I am helpful.	I can do anything I set my mind to.
I am a loving person.	I am confident - I CAN DO IT.
I'm a good listener.	I believe in myself.
I ask good questions.	I can... run fast, read well, etc.

I'm really good at... riding my bike, making friends, math, etc.

I'M LUCKY.

Every problem has an answer.

I'm always in the right place at the right time.

I FEEL HAPPY.

I always make good choices.

Good things happen to me all the time.

I can be whatever I want to be.

I'M GOOD AT BEING ME.

People feel happy when they see me.

I love my life and have lots of fun.

I DO MY BEST ALL THE TIME.

I am unique and special.

mindpower

46

Health Affirmations:

I am healthy and strong.

I'm in great shape.

My body is my best friend.

I FEEL GREAT.

Every day in every way, I am getting better and better.

I feel calm and relaxed (when child is upset).

It is valuable to remind children that affirmations can be said both aloud or silently in their mind. Also, individual words in an affirmation can be emphasized in different ways, so that some words are quieter and others repeated with more enthusiasm. This makes it lots of fun to say. While you can suggest appropriate affirmations to your child, ultimately they must decide which ones "feel right." Often the change of a word or two, or a change of tense, makes the affirmation work more powerfully for them. These adjustments tend to happen naturally as they repeat the affirmations a number of times.

Whatever affirmation your child has chosen, find opportunities to repeat it back to them, *"You're a good swimmer, Danny."* Or, when talking to another adult in Danny's presence, you might say, *"Danny is such an excellent swimmer."* It helps to reinforce the desired image in your child's mind.

On a further note, avoid labeling your child as a "problem child" or repeating such phrases as, "You're always so naughty," or other limiting suggestions. These labels also become imprinted and self-fulfilling, and you end up encouraging the exact behavior you're try-ing to avoid.

As always, be sure to let your child hear *you* use affirmations for numerous situations in your life. Lead by example. Regular use will inspire your children to do the same, especially when they are very young and prone to mimic all of our mannerisms. And in times

If you raise your children to feel that they can accomplish any goal or task they decide upon, you will have succeeded as a parent and you will have given your children the greatest of all blessings.
>> Brian Tracy

of stress, or when your child is facing a challenge, remind him, "Can you use one of your affirmations here?" Or, "What affirmation can you use for this?" Praise and acknowledge your child when she does use an affirmation. "I'm glad you're getting your mind working for you, Sarah." And when affirmations begin to work, as they unquestionably will, be sure to celebrate those instances. "Those affirmations really worked well for you, Nathan. Well done!"

The affirmation technique gives your child a simple but powerful tool they can use for a lifetime. With practice, they will develop the mental habit of using affirmations in a whole range of different situations, resulting in positive attitudes, hope and confidence.

Tips
for Using Affirmations

1 Keep the affirmations short and simple. A short phrase or statement is most effective, like Eloise's, "I am a very good reader."

MIND POWER

2 Always make your sentences positive. Phrase it in such a way that the affirmation is focused on the solution rather than the problem. For example, if your child tells you, "I'm dumb and stupid," you can replace that thinking with a new affirmation such as, "I'm smart," or, "I can do anything." You wouldn't, however, have him repeat, "I'm not dumb and stupid," because, even with the "not" included, the mind still focuses on the negative quality.

3 Don't think you have to force yourself to believe the affirmation when you're saying it. Actually the exact opposite is true. Just by repeating it over and over again it naturally has an effect. Never force it. Relax and sing, chant, shout or whisper your affirmations without thought as to whether they are true or not. The magic of affirmations is that they work automatically, without us having to believe them.

4 Affirmations need to be repeated often, until they become your child's first thought about a situation. Encourage your child to say them over and over again. You might even join in the affirmation, saying it together. "Jessie is smart. Jessie is smart. Jessie is smart." A few minutes a day works well. Bathtime, bedtime and traveling in the car can be great opportunities to work with your children. Bedtime in particular is a wonderful time of the day. A gentle massage on your child's forehead combined with the appropriate affirmation can send your child off to sleep with lovely positive thoughts in his head.

4

VISUALIZATION

Visualization

The technique of visualization is simply one of creating mental pictures of having or doing what it is you desire. Visualization is an excellent technique for children because it utilizes their already active imaginations, giving them an outlet to use their imagination in a positive way. Whether it is passing an exam or making a new friend, this technique can be used with tremendous results.

I was so worried about my math test. Last time I did so lousy even though I knew how to do the questions. I guess I was just nervous or something. This time, Mom got me to practice the exercises where you imagine things in your mind. Every night, for a week before the test, I imagined myself feeling relaxed when I was writing my test and getting all the answers right. Sometimes I would do it in the morning too. I like doing visualizations; they're actually kind of cool. When I wrote my test I felt much better than the last time. And you know what? I scored an 'A'. ›› Kasib, age 10

Children naturally fantasize, daydream and project themselves into unknown situations. A young child, for example, verbalizing a make-believe story, will stretch all boundaries of reality, leading to the most fantastic images and storyline. Imagination in children is highly developed, and they relish the opportunity to use it, so introducing the concept of visualization is easy. It isn't a matter of teaching them what to do, so much as guiding their already lively imaginations into picturing positive outcomes rather than negative ones. You can easily demonstrate to your child how effectively the mind accepts whatever pictures we suggest. Sit down together and practice "painting pictures in your mind." Both of you can close your eyes and make a little game of it.

I'M DOING MY VISUALIZATIONS MOM.

Dad: In my mind, Wendy, I can see you riding on a huge pink elephant.
Wendy: Me too, Daddy. His skin is all wrinkly, and Joni is there too!
Dad: Right, Wendy, and what's Joni doing?
Wendy: She's dancing on the elephant's head.

For younger children, this could lead to having them imagine patting a puppy or a kitten. "Can you feel it lick your hand?" etc. For an older child it could be taking a fantastic space ride in a shuttle, noticing all the controls on the panel as he hurtles through space. Really get into the details. What the child quickly learns is that our imagination is so versatile and agile that it will picture any images that we suggest.

Visualization Games

Here is another easy game you can play with your child to demonstrate how a bit of imagination can improve their performance. Have your child stand with her toes against a line. Then have her jump the longest jump she possibly can, to see how far she can go. Mark the spot where her toes land. Now explain that you are going to try a bit of magic! Have your child, with her eyes either open or closed, imagine doing the jump again, only this time she jumps *even further*. Let her picture in her mind the mark you made where she landed, and then herself landing far past it, and you drawing a new mark. Then let her do it again. Without fail, the second jump is always further. It *is* magic!

The aim is to show your child how her imagination can help to make positive things happen. Your child will quickly recognize the connection between improving her performance in this little game, and her future challenges. Each time your child is faced with a new goal, she will recall the experience of having used visualization techniques successfully in the past. One success builds upon another to create a sense of mastery and empowerment for your child.

The Pointing Game

While Olivia, age eight, was making her final preparation for a tap-dancing competition, I introduced the notion that it was her mind that made her dance as well as she did. While we talked, it became apparent that she disagreed, believing that her success had nothing to do with her mind, but rather with how well she remembered the steps she had been taught.

So Olivia and I played the pointing game, whereby a person endeavors to turn as far as possible in a circular direction while their feet remain firmly planted on the floor. With one arm outstretched, she turned her upper torso to where she thought she couldn't possibly turn any further, and I asked her to make an invisible mark on the wall in line with where her finger was pointing.

Olivia tried her very best and made her first invisible mark about halfway around the room, just past the fireplace. She felt quite proud of what she had achieved, but the more exciting achievement was to follow. Asking Olivia to close her eyes, I had her clearly imagine in her mind pointing almost the full way around the lounge. I then asked her to open her eyes and put into practice what she had just done in her imagination. She passed her first mark by the fireplace, passed her second imaginary mark, and stopped just short of having physically turned the full circle. Her look of surprise and delight was a pleasure to see. She responded, "Gee, Rosie, you're magic." At this point I assured Olivia that it was **her** ability and belief that made it possible.

I then led the discussion to the dancing competitions. I suggest-ed that before she went onstage she could picture herself doing all the steps of her dance perfectly in her mind, and then, when the time came to actually dance for the judges, her mind would help her (because it was her mind that was guiding her dance movements).

While we were dressing her in her dance costume, we made up two affirmations. "I am a beautiful dancer," and "I am a winner," to build positive feelings and to give herself the confidence she would need when competing.

Olivia danced exceptionally well that night, better than she had ever done previously. She also placed well in a couple of cate-gories where the competing dancers were much more experienced.

Olivia and I were both thrilled; Olivia because she did so well, and I because she'd learned a valuable lesson about mind power.
» Rosie, Mind Power presenter.

There is a famous and well-documented experiment conducted by psychologist Alan Richardson that I share in my book *Mind Power Into the 21st Century*. *A group of student basketball players were divided into three groups, tested for their ability to score baskets, and each group's results recorded. The first group was directed to come into the gym every day for a month to practice shooting, the second group was instructed to skip practice altogether, and a third group was instructed to engage in a very different sort of practice. They didn't set foot in the gym at all, but instead stayed in their dorms mentally imagining themselves in the gym practicing. For half an hour each day they "saw" themselves shooting and scoring and improving dramatically. They continued this inner "practice" every day. After a month, the three groups were tested again.*

The first group (those who practiced shooting every day) showed a twenty-four percent improvement in their scores. This second group (those who didn't practice at all) showed no improvement. And the third group – who, remember, had practiced only in their minds – improved equally as much as the group that had practiced for real!

The implications of this are staggering for both us and our children. Visualization gives our children a tool to direct their thoughts towards positive and very tangible results. Not only that, but it's a technique that can be done anytime and anywhere.

There are only two lasting bequests we can hope to give our children. One of these is roots, the other, wings.
» Hodding

A friend of mine's son, Ian, nine years old, recently participated in a triathlon for children. They had to swim 100m, bike 4 kilometers and run 1 kilometer. On the way to the event, he and his mom used the time in the car to talk about Ian doing well in the race, enjoying himself and having lots of energy. He then sat quietly in the back seat and visualized his race. His mom started to talk him through the swim and bike ride, but then he said he wanted to imagine it by himself. So he carried on quietly visualizing the race on his own. Ian swam exceptionally well that day. He felt positive about the bike ride, and ran to the finishing line with energy to spare! Making it through all three segments of such a physically challenging event was a marvelous achievement. The triathlon was a new experience for Ian, and using affirmations and visualization techniques helped give him increased confidence and energy in his efforts. » Nicole

Painting Pictures before Bedtime

Every night just before going to sleep, you can "paint a picture" in your children's minds by having them close their eyes while you tell them a story about themselves. You can choose a different situation each night. It can be an everyday experience like going to the playground, or something special that you expect to have happen in the near future, like starting school or going on a holiday.

Try to "paint" with as many senses as possible, using colors, sounds, smells, tastes, etc. The emphasis is, of course, on how successfully your child handled the situation. There are many times during your child's day when he can practice visualization techniques. Sitting in the doctor's reception room, traveling in a car, waiting in a lineup; there are numerous opportunities to engage your child with this method. In this very simple and gentle way, your children will have learned a new and powerful technique for handling challenging situations.

Whatever your children regularly picture and say to themselves usually comes to pass.

Nine-year-old Valerie came bounding into the house after her diving lesson one night.

"Hey, Daddy, guess what? I did a back dive tonight, for the very first time!"

"Good for you, Val," replied Dad, *"I knew you could do it!"*

"Well, last week I was so scared that I figured I'd never get up the nerve to try. But those visualization exercises must really work. Every night I saw a picture in my mind of me doing a great back dive. I always felt so happy when I did it in my imagination. Tonight I thought about it a lot again. And wow, I just got up there and went for it. Everybody cheered and everything. It was awesome."

There are two main points to remember when using the visualization technique. First, always visualize the circumstances as a real time event happening to you *now*. Visualization is not simply the expression of a desire for something you hope to do in the future. You create images in your mind, using your imagination, seeing and feeling yourself doing it right now. For example, Valerie did not imagine that some day she might be able to do the back dive. In her mind, she saw herself performing it already.

Secondly, put feeling and emotion into the images. Let yourself go, really lose yourself in these make-believe images. One part of your mind will of course know it is not real and just an image, but another part of you will momentarily suspend disbelief and truly get involved. The more the image is repeated in this way, the greater the imprint. This then becomes the blueprint for that circumstance happening.

Rewriting the Script

For children who find themselves unable to forget a troubling event, you can help to change their memory of it. Talk with your child about what she would have preferred to have happen, then have them visualize while you describe a new, desirable outcome for the old situation. There is no good reason for a child to carry with them an old negative memory if it is not serving them well.

"Let's imagine how you might have felt if Roberta could have stayed for dinner tonight instead of having to go to her sister's track meet? Let's make up the happy ending that could happen next time we invite her."

Give them a new, positive memory for that situation and it will serve as a blueprint for future experiences. This is also a great opportunity for you to introduce to your children new social skills, simply by having them imagine themselves using them.

Picture Power for Scary Dreams and Nightmares

In the chapter on affirmations we mentioned the effectiveness of visual signs or symbols. Mental pictures also have the same power to affect our subconscious expectations, and to help bring them to fruition. Following is another story about a young girl in a Mind Power for Children program who *drew* her fears away.

> *We must teach our children to dream with their eyes open.*
> » Harry Edwards

Koto, my five-year-old daughter, learned to 'change the picture' of her nightmares. When she had a bad dream, together we would sit down and change the end of it into something positive and funny. Then Koto would draw a picture of the positive dream and stick it on the wall beside her bed where she would see it often. This became a habit, and now she knows she can change the bad dream into a positive picture in her mind any time she wants."

» Akiko

A Visualization of Abundance to Teach Your Children

This visualization can be done with eyes open or closed. The goal is to get children to look at all the positive qualities they can invite into their lives.

First draw a picture of six containers of any shape or size. Then repeat to your child in a calm slow voice, using your own words, *"Close your eyes if you like, or watch the picture. Visualize the sun shining down on you. You can feel the warmth of its rays and the lovely, clear white light shining over your whole body. You feel calm and relaxed and very happy.*

On a shelf above your head are the containers you have drawn, filled with wonderful things that can happen to you. There is a container filled with friendship. Imagine that container pouring down over you, showering you with lots of wonderful friends. There is a container filled with love and kindness. Imagine that container pouring love and kindness all over you, showering you with love and kindness all through your life.

Now imagine the container labeled 'good health' being poured over your whole body. Feel all the good health soaking into your whole body.

Next, the container filled with pocket money is showering over you. The container of pocket money is always filled to the brim and pours out plenty of money whenever you want. Imagine it pouring out into your hands now.

Now the container of happiness is showering over you. Happiness is pouring over your head and soaking into your whole body.

There is one last container sitting on the shelf above you, and it's the container of abundance. Abundance means plenty of everything you want. Imagine tipping up the container of abundance and pouring it over your head. Plenty of everything you want. All through your life you will have plenty of everything because you can feel the abundance showering down over you and filling your life with good things."

> **The real magic wand is the child's own mind.**
> » Jose Ortega Y Gasset

Create whatever other containers you want, filled with any number of wonderful things. Tip up those containers and shower all the good feelings down over you.

It doesn't matter what you or your children call it: visualization, mental rehearsal, painting a picture or magical thinking. The important point is that it works. Once your child has been introduced to this technique and has experienced successful results several times, they will naturally use it as future opportunities arise.

Tips

for Using Visualization

1

MIND POWER

Be sure to have your children visualize their goal as if it is happening to them *now*. Check that the vocabulary and imagery used supports the "now" energy you are working with. Remember, visualizing anything as a future event keeps the goal in the future. Visualizing it as a real time "now" event, imagining it happening right now, sets in motion the reality of it happening. A subtle but important difference.

2

Encourage them to put lots of *detail* and *feeling* into the visualization. Doing a visualization is an exhilarating experience. It feels great. In fact, you can use this as a guide to how well your children are doing the practice. If they feel positive and uplifted after the process, they're doing it right!

3 Always visualize the *outcome* of your goal as having already happened. Often visualizations become reality in highly unusual and surprising ways, so it is best not to worry about *how* they are going to happen. Concentrate on the end result without concerning yourself with the details.

4 Doing a visualization can involve everything from a slow, almost photo-by-photo process, to a fast-forward speed through. Often in the beginning, when working with something new, it can take time for the mind to download all the information, thoughts and feelings. Sometimes a number of reruns and cuts are needed before the visualized scene feels and looks right. Each child becomes a young Stephen Spielberg in the process.

Tips
for Using Visualization

MIND POWER

5 Your child can visualize with her eyes either open or closed. Both methods work well, and it's really just a matter of preference. Your child may choose to alternate between the two. Also some children will experience the "feeling" more than the actual inner pictures, and vice versa. Again, both ways work.

6 Remind your child to *repeat* their visualization often. Each time the images are repeated they become clearer and more potent. Think of these exercises as mental vitamin pills and do them daily. Repetition focuses the child's mind on the positive outcome. It also builds confidence, which allows children to make positive choices that lead to the attainment of their goals.

VISUALIZATION

5

ACKNOWLEDGING

Acknowledging

In our busy lives, children are sometimes only noticed when they are misbehaving. When they act up, make a mistake, bring home a poor report card, make too much noise or squabble with their siblings, we're always there to let them know about it. But positive behavior should also be acknowledged. More than just praising compliant behavior, we want to acknowledge our children's constructive qualities and the ever-present goodness of them just being themselves.

Children are naturally positive and upbeat about who they are, but criticism or ridicule from parents, teachers or friends can make even a young person doubt herself. Children achieve countless successes every day; let us take the time to acknowledge them for as many of these successes as possible. Providing the praise is sincere, it's inconceivable that we could ever acknowledge a child too much.

Ordinary Children Are Extraordinary

Acknowledging is a technique that helps children feel worthy and special. We do this by bringing to their attention areas where they are presently or have previously been successful. Reminding children of their achievements increases their confidence and reinforces their self-worth. It creates a vibration of success and confidence *now* in their life, and inspires them to undertake new challenges with enthusiasm.

"Mom, Sebastian says I'm stupid and I paint like a baby!" cries four-year-old Jordan from the bedroom.

"Oh dear, Jordan," responds Mom coming into his room, "it sounds like that big brother of yours is having a miserable day and trying to take it out on you. I was just telling your teacher how delighted I am with all of the beautiful paintings you have been bringing home each week. The colors on this one in particular, (she says pointing to the wall) are so bright, I feel happy just looking at it. I'm a very lucky Mom to live with such a talented artist!" (And she gives Jordan a big hug.)

The child who is loved uncon-ditionally and acknowledged fre-quently feels secure, strong, and has the necessary courage to move into unpredictable and unknown situations freely. His creativity, intelligence and emotional development will flourish. He will feel special, worthy and will have the confidence to venture on to greater challenges, which in turn will augment his growth even further.

Acknowledging can start before birth, and continue from your child's first day throughout the rest of his life. Welcome your child into the world; tell him how special he is and how much you love him. Invite those people who will play an important role in your child's life to speak their acknowledgements to your newborn, blessing him with qualities that will support him throughout his life. Your baby's brain will access and retain this information in his memory for future reference. Subconsciously he will pick up on all this loving energy.

The effect that our thoughts, feelings and words have upon a child's subconscious must never be underestimated. This ability provides parents and caregivers a tremendous opportunity to imprint positive and lasting feelings of worthiness upon a child at a very early age. At every stage of her growth we can supply our child with feelings of self-worth and uniqueness, thereby helping her build a self-image that will allow her to overcome any obstacle, setback or criticism.

Building a Positive Self-Image

A child's self-image is formed very early in her life. By the time she is seven or eight, it is already well along to being established. A whole host of beliefs and assumptions about herself are already internalized as she interprets and reacts to her ever-changing environment. A child's self-image will continue to fluctuate and ebb and flow as she matures, but the foundation is being laid at a very early age.

Muriem's List

Muriem's school day was almost over. "Just before you go home tonight, everyone," called out her teacher, "I want to congratulate Sophie for her excellent contribution to the community science fair yesterday. Her project won first prize for her age group." Everyone clapped and Sophie looked very proud. "I also want you to wish Jeremy the best for tomorrow when he competes in the junior tennis championships," added the teacher. "We're all very proud of you both! Now off you go and have a terrific weekend, everybody."

MURIEM'S LIST

I'm good at being friendly
I'm good at riding my bike
I'm good at drawing horses

Muriem walked home with her friend Elly. "Do you want to come over to my place to play when we get home, El?" asked Muriem. "Sorry, I can't today," replied Elly. "I've got to practice my piano."

Muriem went inside her house, plunked down her schoolbag and looked around for her mother, who she found talking on the phone to Grandma Walstein. "Isn't that wonderful?" her mother was saying, "Jacob must be a fabulous chess player to get into the top level at his age."

Muriem poured herself some juice from the fridge and sat down at the kitchen table. When her mother was finished her call, Muriem walked slowly into the living room, plopped herself onto the sofa and said to her mother, "Mom, everyone is good at something except me. Elly's good at the piano, Sophie's smart at science, and Jeremy's probably the best tennis player in our school. Now my cousin Jacob is on the top chess team. I'm no good at anything!"

"Just a minute," exclaimed her mother, "I think you're good at many things. How about you sit right here and write down all the things you do really well."

Muriem felt completely stumped – she couldn't think of a

single thing. Finally, her mother offered to help. "Muriem, on garbage collection day, you were the only one in our whole family who remembered to put the trash bags out. Without you, our garbage would never have been collected. Put that down on your list." Muriem didn't think remembering the garbage was such a big deal, but she wrote it down. "Another thing you are very good at is you always know when I'm tired and need some help or even a hug when I'm upset. That's very special to me because not everyone notices."

> **True self-esteem emerges from knowing one is truly loved.**
> » Paul Coleman

"Gee, I didn't know that was very special," thought Muriem as she wrote that down on her list, too.

"Now you think of some things you're good at yourself," her mother suggested. Muriem thought for a few moments and wrote down:

I'm good at riding a bike.
I'm good at being friendly.
I'm good at remembering to feed my pets.
I'm good at drawing horses.

In the end she thought of twelve different things she was good at. "I'm actually pretty good at a lot of things," thought Muriem, rather pleased, and she told her mother.

"Way to go!" said Muriem's mother. "Why don't you put that list up on your bedroom wall, and if you're feeling discouraged again, you'll be able to look at all the important things you're really good at."

Acknowledging List

You can read Muriem's story to your children, or make up one yourself. Once your children realize everyone has special qualities, you can ask them to make a list of all the things they're good at, making suggestions if necessary, but encouraging them to come up with the list on their own. Some prompting questions can help when they are stuck.

What do you think you do that makes you an awesome person?
What things do you do that help your friends / other people / family / school?
What things can you do all by yourself?
What things are you getting better at doing each day?
What are some things that other people love about you?

Dad: As I recall, you received a certificate at your piano recital last week. What does that tell you?
Josh: That's true. Third place. I guess I'm pretty good at piano, huh?
Dad: I'd certainly say so. Make sure to write that down. And how about the project you've been working on all afternoon?
Josh: My MK7 water bomber? You know, my teacher said I'm the best

model builder in the class. I'm gonna put that at the top of my list. And so on...

Following are some fun activities that utilize the techniques of acknowledging in a variety of ways. Together with your children, choose to integrate each technique according to their own individual personalities and learning styles. Working with your child's natural strengths will make the practice both more enjoyable and successful.

For instance, your child may be a visual learner, naturally observant and eager to see things with his "own eyes." Maybe your child is an auditory learner, verbally adept and a keen listener to sounds, voices and music. Or perhaps, your child is especially kinesthetic, able to express ideas and feelings freely with her body. Although most children learn through a combination of these styles, one is bound to stand out a bit more. Each child is different, with her own special kind of "genius." We can use this understanding to help our children reach their maximum potential.

A list of your child's accomplishments is a terrific visual reminder for your child, and everyone else, to see. Simple everyday achievements that we might normally take for granted can be included on the list, and will also serve as a source of pride and satisfaction for your child. A big, bold, colorful banner praising your son or daughter's positive qualities is a powerful message. An acknowledging list can be posted in a prominent place for everyone to see, or more privately in your child's bedroom. You can even make your list on a portable chart, poster, mobile or box, that can move around the house with your child.

"I call it my 'A' list and it's got lots of stickers and cool stuff on it." » Andrew, 8.

Hall of Fame

Every child can have a "Hall of Fame" where past successes can be remembered and acknowledged. Whether through mom and dad's recollections, or storytelling sessions over the photo album, reminiscing over "treasured moments" in your child's history will provide endless hours of family enjoyment.

"When you were a baby you always laughed and smiled every time you saw me looking at you."

"When you were learning to walk you were always so brave and courageous. No matter how many times you fell you got up and tried again. You're a very persistent person who knows how to accomplish things."

"When you were four you climbed all the way to the top of the jungle gym in the schoolyard. Nothing could stop you."

Even as an adult, the combination of storytelling and the sharing of photos can ignite the most powerful feelings. Everyone present will be nurtured by this process, so make time to enjoy this activity on a regular basis.

Surprise Acknowledging Lists

This is a simple way your child can be guided into noticing the uniqueness of others. Perhaps your husband has been working late most nights, finishing off an important project. Take your young daughter aside and say:

"You know Daddy has been working really hard lately and sometimes he's been a bit grumpy, hasn't he? Why don't we surprise him with an acknowledging list and put it on his desk? Let's think of lots of reasons why we think he's the best Daddy in the world."

Doing this helps the child to focus on positive qualities of others. It's fun, thoughtful, and imagine the surprise when the lucky recipient finds the list.

Your child will learn from your example how rewarding it is to praise and acknowledge others. You can do this for grandma, grandpa, aunts and uncles, friends, teachers – anyone your child has contact with.

Over the years we've seen hundreds of mother and father's day cards designed and composed by children in preschool through to grade six. The children who weren't yet writing often came to us for help to print some of the most endearing words ever expressed about a parent.

"I love my dad because: he's the coolest ever; he has a beard like Santa Claus; he lets us have popcorn ... even when it isn't 'treat day'; he tells me the funniest stories – they make me fall on the floor; he can give great big bear hugs!"

Perhaps the most touching aspect of the card making was the reaction of a parent who told us, *"You know, my son's card came on a day when I was wondering if I really could do anything RIGHT as a parent. It's amazing what our children remember even though we may have forgotten."*

Modeling Self-Acknowledgement

If you have been led to believe that saying something complimentary about yourself is bigheaded or just not done, toss that belief aside. This activity can in fact be very rewarding, in several different ways. By looking for opportunities to acknowledge our own special qualities, we are teaching our children that self-praise is

84

mindpower

important. Yes it is! And our accomplishments don't have to be earth shattering in order for them to be worthy of acknowledgement either. So why not get into the habit of regularly patting ourselves on the back?

> *We worry about what a child will be tomorrow, yet we forget that he is someone today.*
> ›› Stacia Tauscher

"*I just remembered Uncle Leonard's birthday in time. Call me 'Super-memory'!*"

"*Look at all that ironing! Have you ever seen ironing done to such a state of perfection before?*"

Silly? Not at all. You'll be amazed at how good it makes you feel, and because children pick up so easily on anything positive, it'll be a habit they're sure to copy. Children love to think that their parents are special people, so be liberal with the self-praise.

Recently a parent visited me regarding her twelve-year-old stepson. Did I have any suggestions for creating a positive attitude? After our conversation, there were several ideas she was keen to try. A few weeks later I saw her again. She told me that she decided to start off her campaign by writing positive words beside her own name on a big poster and pinning it on the family notice board. She wrote:

*J - Joyful **U** - Unique **L** - Liberated **I** - Intelligent **E** - Exceptional*

Her stepson noticed and was heard to comment that she was into that weird stuff again. Julie smiled quietly to herself and went out shopping. What did she discover when she returned but that all three of the children were hard at work making up their own posters. Julie had not had to say a word. » Carla

Elephant Ears Acknowledging

Every parent soon learns that little children have very "big" ears. They like to listen in on adult conversations, and their ears perk up at the very mention of their own name. We can take shameless advantage of this tendency, if we think our child is listening, by giving them something worth listening to. In your conversation with grandma or your neighbor, acknowledge your child, mentioning his accomplishments at music, spelling or skiing, including how proud of him you are. You can

YOU SHOULD
HAVE SEEN
HOW HOLLY...

rest assured that the message is being absorbed, and that his confidence is being bolstered. This avenue is particularly useful if your child has difficulty accepting compliments directly.

The Acknowledging Game

This activity is perfect for birthday parties or afternoon get-togethers. Gather a group of children in a circle. Write every child's name on a piece of paper and put these into a hat. Each child takes a turn at drawing a name from the hat and then, keeping the name a surprise, mimes an admirable quality about that child. For instance, Chelsea picks Robert's name from the hat. Chelsea then stands in the circle and mimes how skilled Robert is at skiing, or that Robert is healthy and strong. The children all try to guess what the attribute is and who she is pretending to be.

Sample Acknowledgements

- *I acknowledge you for remembering to feed the dog all on your own.*
- *You have a great memory.*
- *I acknowledge the effort you made at Sports Day today. You tried lots of new activities and you were very supportive of your friends' efforts as well.*
- *I acknowledge how patient you were while we waited so long in the bank lineup today.*
- *I acknowledge how you remembered to set your alarm to wake up early for your track meet.*

- *I acknowledge how kind you were with your baby brother this morning when he was feeling sick.*
- *I acknowledge you for remembering that garbage pickup day was changed to Friday this week. I totally forgot.*

Even the most difficult child has special qualities worth acknowledging. Be doubly sure you search them out and acknowledge them. Be vigilant in your effort to acknowledge behavior that you would also like her to have, when you see it happen! If your two children tend to bicker, let them overhear you mention how impressed you were to notice them playing cooperatively with one another, how great it is to hear them discussing their differences; how intelligent they have been to work out a win-win solution. All children have the ability to do all these things, and sometimes indirectly drawing your children's attention to positive behavior is sufficient to motivate them to exhibit it more often.

A word of advice though. Be subtle, be truthful, and don't overdo it. Acknowledging needs to be sincere. Children can sense when you are being dishonest, so if you don't believe your child has a particular quality, you are better to focus on other positive qualities that they possess. One can build upon another. The amazing psychology of human nature is that the more your children hear and see their positive qualities being recognized, the more motivated and empowered they become to add to those qualities.

[
Acknowledging increases motivation

Acknowledging improves a child's self-esteem

Acknowledging gives children self-confidence

Acknowledging teaches children to trust their decisions

Acknowledging motivates children to seek goals

Acknowledging develops responsibility
]

I'M UNIQUE
AND
SPECIAL

Tips
for Using Acknowledging

1

MIND POWER

Use balance and creativity when acknowledging. Our children's worthiness isn't just connected with stellar performance, or how well they do something. Participation, effort and enjoyment are equally important and deserve equal credit. Remember to express appreciation for your child's accomplishments beyond the obvious certificates and prizes. Activities such as learning to ride a bike, giving the dog a bath, or finding a lost earring also warrant attention.

2

Acknowledgements are used to help your child feel pleased with her life right now. Bring to your child's attention past and present accomplishments regularly. Remind her that she is already successful in many areas of her life, regardless of how she may presently feel. Too often temporary setbacks make a young person doubt herself, but with our consistent reinforcement of her positive qualities, she will bounce back quickly.

3 Acknowledging consists of noticing activities and actions. While it is true that children are wonderful simply because of who they are, all of us need more than that to hang our feelings of success upon. The success vibration should be related to some tangible attitude, effort, or action.

4 Be creative with your methods of acknowledging. Falling into the pattern of acknowledging with just one method, while beneficial, won't be nearly as effective as using a variety of ways to build your child's self-esteem.

5 Acknowledge yourself regularly. Not only will this be wonderful modeling for your child, but it will also pick you up, often when you need it the most. Let's remind ourselves regularly that in spite of all our shortcomings and difficulties, we are loving and supportive parents.

6

ELIMINATING NEGATIVES

Eliminating Negatives

Negative thoughts can come out of nowhere and be about anything. Even the most positive child will find herself worrying sometimes, and a negative child will often fall into the pattern of constantly worrying. Worrying is what happens when the mind projects us into some future situation, and we begin to imagine all the things that could go wrong. While it's true that anticipating future possibilities and preparing to deal with them can be helpful, if left unchecked, this fantasizing can easily spin out of control.

Negatives can also result from dwelling on unpleasant past experiences, instances where we failed or were hurt in some way. Dwelling on these types of thoughts inevitably saps our energy.

"My mom says I'm a worry-wart, just like my dad."
 » *Stuart, age three*

Worries too often become self-fulfilling, propelling us towards the things we fear most. That's the cruel reality of negative thinking. The images we consistently dwell on, whether positive or negative, reflect the circumstances we tend to attract in our life. This being the case, the practice of eliminating negatives is a highly desirable process. Talk to your children about the difference between positive and negative thinking. Ask them what advantage, if any, there is to thinking negatively. They might actually come up with some. Listen to them, commenting and correcting any misconceptions. Together you will conclude that positive thinking is always better.

It is easier and wiser to raise a happy, healthy child than to repair an adult.
>> Christina Bublick

Once everyone agrees on this point, the teaching part is easy and fun. Children want to think positive thoughts; they just need to be shown how. Instill in your children the understanding that their mind is their best friend.

"Your mind will help you achieve any goal you have. It is so creative and powerful that it will think whatever thought you choose for it."

Emotional Coaching

"One morning I had just brought my three-year-old daughter home from a morning at preschool and was busy preparing lunch. I popped a dish of pasta into the microwave oven and was about to close the oven door when my daughter announced that she wished to complete that particular task. Unwilling to break the momentum of my hurried preparation, or to lift her to the required height, I said something casual like, "Next time," and closed the door. Well, the tears flowed copiously. Through

the most heart-wrenching wails she sobbed, "I didn't get to be the "special helper" at preschool and now I didn't get to do that either!" >> Ric

Children see and feel the world through a different lens than adults, and their immediate emotional range is stunning. A toddler can go from fits of ecstasy to howls of anguish and back to contentment in what seems like the blink of an eye. Even a ten-year-old can turn what we would see as a minor irritation into a profound emotional crisis.

"My favorite pajamas aren't clean and I'm going to Janie's for a sleep-over tonight!"

Emotions and thoughts go hand in hand. If we want our children to be happy and think positive thoughts, we need to help them understand their emotions.

Emotions are like waves on the ocean. They rise and fall. Sometimes they're stormy and sometimes they're calm. These emotional waves are temporary, ever changing. Our challenge as humans is to ride the waves, like a skilled surfer, rather than be swamped by them. It is important to remember that beyond the wildest wave there is always a tranquil place within us.

Thinking of yourself as an emotional coach helps to expand your vision of what it means to be a parent. Emotional coaching means helping your child to recognize and name his own emotions, to recognize what is behind the feeling – angry, sad, frightened. All of these emotions have their roots in past experiences. Communicating and sharing your feelings together can help. Gradually your child will understand the causes of his emotions and learn to recognize the difference between feelings, thoughts and actions. The next step, through coaching and encouragement, is to help him discover that he can choose different thoughts and reactions to deal with life's countless difficulties and disappointments, as well as the successes and triumphs.

Encourage your children to say, *"I have a choice. I can let this situation bother me; I can allow myself to feel angry / sad / scared / confused / vengeful, etc., but I don't have to. Instead, I can choose to feel another way - optimistic / happy / sure of myself, etc. Every situation gives me choices."*

Teaching our children about their feelings and the implications of their thinking will guide them through their emotional growth. Be patient and understanding. Lessons often have to be learned again and again. Emotions are volatile. When we adults are upset we sometimes say, "I can't think straight." If emotions can interfere with *our* logic, how much more so in a child whose emotions are jumping wildly all over the place? Eventually our emotional coaching will show results, and our children will reap immense benefit from it. It's hard work and sometimes you wonder if they're ever going to learn, but with your patience and coaching they will. It's certainly worth the effort.

Two terrific times for talking about feelings with your children are at bedtime and while driving in the car. Many children choose bedtime to finally "wind-down" enough to let their feelings settle into a sharing framework. Earlier in the day they were "too busy feeling them!" It makes sense. An inviting sentence like, "Tell me about your day ..." can bring about surprising results. A good idea is to count twelve seconds in your head, *before* jumping in. We adults are often tempted to fill in the gap of silence while our child is still considering what to say. Spending a few extra moments at your child's bedside while they "download" their feelings is precious time well spent.

The family vehicle can also be an ideal time for sharing and avoiding frustration. Cars provide a quiet, private, comparatively safe space for discussing any of your children's thoughts or feelings about what's going on in their lives, and are definitely high on our list of possible teachable moments.

Negative Thoughts Are Like Weeds in Our Garden

An easy way to explain to children how to eliminate negative thoughts is to compare our mind to a garden. Children can easily understand this analogy, and it encourages them to be diligent gardeners.

Our mind is like a garden. And in our garden are both flowers and weeds. Flowers are the positive thoughts and there are many different types of them, just like there are many different flowers. Each one is different and looks different and smells different. The same applies to negative thoughts; there are many different types of these negative thoughts, and they are like weeds. Weeds will choke out the flowers if there are too many of them. So, just like a gardener who pulls out the weeds in his garden, we weed out the negative thoughts from our "inner garden." It's good to do a little bit of gardening every day. It keeps us feeling happy and confident.

An important first step in eliminating negatives is to help children distinguish between positive and negative thoughts. A simple guide is for them to ask themselves, "How do I feel?" Positive thoughts make us feel good, happy and content with ourselves. Negative thoughts are those that make us feel uncertain, sad or unhappy about ourselves. How do we feel? That's the key. Our feelings tell us a lot.

ELIMINATING NEGATIVES

Whenever your children find themselves feeling sad, worried, or frustrated, they can ask themselves, "Am I thinking positive or negative thoughts," and if they're thinking negative thoughts they can change them. It's as simple as that. We can change any thought in our mind anytime we want. Our mind is our private garden and we are the gardeners.

Parent: Can you think of some examples of negative thoughts?

Child: Well ... I can't do anything right.

Parent: That's pretty negative, alright. How does it make you feel?

Child: Awful.

Parent: You see, your feelings can be your guide to help you find those negative weed thoughts. Now how about some positive thoughts?

Child: I like myself.

Parent: That's the way. You're really good at telling the difference between positive and negative thoughts. How do you feel when you think positive thoughts?

Child: Good and happy.

Parent: That's right. So why would anyone think negative thoughts if they don't have to?

Child: I don't know.

Parent: Because just like weeds, negative thoughts can appear out of nowhere, when you least expect them. So, as smart and happy gardeners, we are always looking out *to make sure negative weed thoughts haven't snuck back into our garden while we weren't looking. It's a good idea to do a little bit of weeding every day.*

Surefire Techniques to Weed Out Negative Thoughts

The "Switch"

This technique teaches children that they have emotional options. While feeling badly about an adverse situation may be your child's *first* reaction, it doesn't have to stay that way. So, when your child gets stuck, let them know that they have an invisible switch inside their minds that turns on positive thoughts and feelings. If they seem to be locked into negativity, remind them, *"It's time to turn on the switch."*

It is important that your child learn how to change his emotional state before he starts making rash decisions or taking hasty action. The "switch" technique is all about transforming negative emotions into positive thoughts and energy. This is not about changing the situation; the situation stays the same. What changes is our reaction, thoughts and feelings.

Constructive Activity

"But Mommy, no good thoughts are coming through."

Reassure your child that when the switch is on, positive thoughts

mindpower

will come through, but sometimes we have to be patient and listen especially carefully for them. There are always positive thoughts inside us waiting to be discovered.

You can suggest that while waiting, she might put away her toys or help dad clean the car. Giving a child something else to do and think about shifts the focus away from the problem, and is frequently an effective way to change negative emotional energy into constructive physical activity. And, of course, the accomplishment of a useful task generates additional positive feelings.

Changing the Video

If the current situation is generating negative thoughts or emotions, we can teach our children to think of it as watching a B-grade movie. We'd all much rather watch an A-grade movie, so why not just mentally change the video. With our imagination we can take out the old video and replace it with the same characters, but a different, far more enjoyable script. Rewrite the scene and visualize a successful outcome to the situation.

Help your child to keep his expectations positive because expectations have a tendency to become self-fulfilling prophecies. What our children think about and expect is often what they will encounter, so as parents we encourage our children to play lots of super A-grade movies in their imaginations.

Why not have a mental library chock full of them!

Parents of young children can use nighttime to create stories where their child is the hero, handling a topical issue with great competence. Your child, the hero, never panics, always maintains his cool, is invariably calm and collected. He is never confused and always knows the right thing to do. He is never angry and always looks for alternatives when things go wrong. Rather than being vengeful, he is compassionate and helps his adversaries.

Fill your children's imaginations with positive, emotional and physical behavior. Seeing themselves as heroes who can move quickly out of negative emotional states, rising triumphantly above their circumstances, gives them terrific role models to follow. Teach them that they never need to be victims of either their inner or outer experiences. They always have the power to change what they don't like because they can change their thoughts.

The "Cannonball" Method

Have your child take some deep breaths and relax. Talk them through a guided visualization where they imagine the negative thought as a black cannonball.

"Put it in the cannon. Fire the cannon and shoot the ball high into

the sky out over the ocean. Watch it hit the water and sink out of sight. You can picture yourself as the captain of a sailing ship, and if the negative thought comes back, order it back into the cannon and fire it off again. It's lots of fun. Imagine the cannon-ball sinking to the very bottom of the ocean, where it belongs. You can even imagine it landing with a thud or disappearing in the slimy mud to be lost forever."

Once they pick up on how to do it, children love to cannonball their negatives away.

The "Opposite Thought" Method

Counteract the negative with the exact opposite thought. If your child has a negative thought, such as, "I have no friends," encourage him to put the opposite thought in his mind – "I have many friends." We can think whatever thoughts we choose, even if they're not yet real. So pick a thought that is the exact opposite of the negative thought. Mind power techniques train our minds to do this. Your son is worried about doing poorly on a test? What's the exact opposite? "Passing the test with an excellent grade." So encourage him to begin thinking those thoughts. When you concentrate on the new, positive thought for a few minutes, the negative thought is chased away. Sometimes you will have to chase the negative thought away many times, just like a pesky fly that keeps landing on your arm, but remind your child that he is always smarter and more powerful than any of those negative thoughts.

Using Affirmations

Affirmations are extremely effective for transforming negative thoughts in our mind. Your child can affirm that he'll learn to do the backstroke, play the piano, or enjoy summer camp; that he'll do whatever the negative thought is telling him won't happen. Share with your child that negatives hate positive affirmations; that they'll fly from his mind when he uses affirmations, like a bat recoiling from sunlight. *"When you use your positive affirmations the negatives will quickly flee from your secret power."* Positive affirmations are always more powerful than negative thoughts.

A favorite children's story of ours is "The Kite," from *Frog and Toad Are Friends,* by Arnold Lobel. Frog and Toad went out to fly their kite. A group of nearby birds looked on rather skeptically, mocking Frog and Toad and telling them their kite would never fly. Frog and Toad tried and tried – each time without success. They had a "running" try and then a "running and leaping" try. Each time the kite landed on the ground with a thump, much to the delight of the teasing birds. Each time Toad became more and more discouraged, wanting to give up on the kite. Frog, on the other hand, kept insisting that they try one more thing. Finally, after a "running, leaping and shouting" try, the kite zoomed into the air to the amazement of Frog and Toad. Even the birds couldn't fly as high as the kite that day! Negatives are exactly like those pesky birds. They make a lot of noise and try to discourage us, but if we persist with our techniques they'll fly away.

Worry is not only an unpleasant experience, but it adversely affects the way our children perform as well. In numerous studies it has been found that the more prone a person is to worrying, the poorer his academic performance. The very act of worrying uses up mental resources that could otherwise be used for processing information. You cannot worry and access correct answers from your mind at the same time.

IMAGINE YOURSELF RIDING LIKE A PRO.

In one study, a group of adult non-worriers were asked to worry on purpose for fifteen minutes, and their ability to do tasks they had previously accomplished without difficulties deteriorated substantially. Little wonder that positive students do better than negative ones. Saying to your child, "Don't worry!" means quite the opposite, since it evokes images of worrying. Instead teach her the skills to turn worry into a positive expectation. Good moods, confidence and positive expectations are the prerequisites for successful outcomes in school, sports, making friends, and in life itself.

Always encourage your child to think about what he wants to happen, as opposed to what he's afraid might happen. Fears, worries or feelings of unhappiness are signals to let us know we're thinking negative thoughts. If a negative thought is allowed to repeat itself over and over again, it gains power, becomes bold and persistent, but remind your child that every negative thought knows that we're the boss, and that it must always listen to what we say.

Visualizations to Help Your Child Eliminate Negatives

It is very common for children to have a special blanket or toy that they keep close at hand as a symbol of power and protection. Since the time of the cave dwellers, people have worn amulets, beads, crystals and much more as protective "armor" against "bad luck" or "evil spirits." For four-year-old Andrea, it was a wooden sword that she and her dad had made for her pirate costume at Halloween. Carrying that sword, Andrea felt like a powerful pirate, and so for many months it lay across the end of her bed, "keeping her safe."

A few years later, the time finally came when she passed on her wooden sword to another younger pirate. This is a very beneficial method for combating fears in young children. An older child, however, will find a mind power visualization more effective, and something they can carry within them at all times.

Six-year-old Joel was worried about an upcoming fire drill at school. He was sure he was going to get lost and disoriented. It got to the point where Joel started waking up at night with scary dreams about being caught in the hallway, unable to make it to the safe refuge spot in the school playground. Even though his teacher carefully explained the safety procedures to the class, Joel was anxious and unsure. His mom suggested that together they create a visualization to help relieve his anxiety. Several times a day, and especially before falling to sleep, Joel visualized himself and his friends stepping up calmly from their desks, walking together down the long corridor, out the exit door and to the safe refuge spot. In his mind he imagined himself feeling relaxed and brave, walking steadily and calmly along his route and exiting easily with the others. He decided to name this visualization the "Getting Out

Safely Movie." As the days passed, Joel's anxiety waned and he start-ed looking forward to the drill ahead. When the day of the evacua-tion practice finally came, it went off without a hitch. Joel was thrilled. "It was just like my 'mind movie,' only in real life. I practiced it so many times, I wasn't even scared," he said proudly.

Your children, like Joel, can learn to create visualization exercis-es to prepare them for any general concerns or fears. An excellent and all-purpose visualization exercise is creating an "energy shield" against negative situations and anxiety.

Creating Your Very Own "Energy Shield"

An "energy shield" is an invisible protective covering that emanates from the child herself. It's a metaphor for personal pow-er, strong will and resolute determination. Here's how an "energy shield" can be created.

Before you start, find a quiet space where your child can sit com-fortably. Suggest that he take three deep breaths and close his eyes. You can talk him through the experience using these or similar words.

Take one more deep breath and really relax your body. Feel your toes relax ... feel your legs relax ... feel your hips and bottom relax ... feel your tummy relax ... feel your arms and hand relax ... feel your shoulders and neck relax ... feel your head relax ... feel your whole body relax. You feel very comfort-

> **The values, beliefs and habits you instill in your child now will become the foundation they'll use forever.**
> ›› Sylvia Bak

able. Now imagine taking yourself off to a magic place ... it may be an island, a beautiful magic island. This island is called the Island of Calmness because no one is ever upset or unhappy here. You can do lots of special things on this island. See yourself doing some of these special things, like swimming in the water or maybe playing with friends, and eating yummy food. Feel the peace and the fun of this Island of Calmness. Everything is happy, beautiful and peaceful.

Imagine there is a protective energy shield all around your island. You can see it in your mind's eye. You can feel it with your body. This energy shield only lets in good things ... love and happy thoughts and friendly people. **Nothing** can get through this shield unless you invite it in. The energy shield is very powerful. Storms of all sorts can rage around you, but you are on the Island of Calmness and you are completely protected because you have an energy shield.

You also have a very powerful energy shield around your body.

Imagine a glistening, invisible energy shield around your whole body.

Now, just for a second, imagine that somebody has said something unkind to you, something cruel and hurtful. Perhaps someone has shouted at you. You begin to feel hurt and upset ... but suddenly ... you remember your energy shield. Your energy shield is all around you, and so the unkind remarks just bounce off. The hurtful words can't get through; the shouting doesn't affect you at all. You remain calm and confident.

See yourself calm, relaxed and confident. Upsets can't reach you ... because you have an energy shield. Your energy shield stays with you always and is completely invisible ... but very powerful. Whenever you are in a situation that might upset you, you can put up your energy shield and see yourself smiling and confident behind it.

Feel yourself being calm and confident in any situation. It feels great. When you are calm and confident you always do just the right thing. Now you see how beautifully clear and vibrant your mind's picture is; how bold and bright the colors are. Notice how you can even turn the colors up brighter, like on your television.

When you're ready, start to move your toes and fingers. Gently stretch your body, open your eyes and think about your energy shield.

mindpower

112

Energy shields are great for protecting your children from name calling or teasing, or to simply make them feel confident and inspired.

Both positive and negative patterns of thinking become well entrenched by the time a child reaches adolescence. Even a five-year-old will have well-developed thinking habits, so teaching your child to eliminate negative thoughts early is one of the most important things we can do as parents. With practice, your children will learn to identify negative thoughts at an earlier point in their distress. They will also be able to figure out why they're feeling the way they are, and what thoughts are responsible for these feelings. With skills to remove the thoughts that are making them feel negative, they can begin thinking positively, and feeling better, any time they choose.

Tips
for Eliminating Negatives

1 Check in with your child when they express their worries. Teach them how to *transform* those annoying negative thoughts into positive expectations. Persistent negatives can fester and grow into a serious concern if left unchecked, so we want to address them early and effectively. A negative thought only has as much power as we choose to give it.

2 Model for your children how you, too, use these techniques to rid yourself of niggling doubts and negativity. Children are very empathetic and will learn to be more objective about their own feelings when they see you share yours. Naturally, you will want to limit your examples to fairly insignificant worries rather than major problems, which could potentially undermine your child's sense of personal security.

mindPower

(114)

3 When you find your children worrying, suggest one of the techniques, "Brian, why don't you cannonball it," or "Sanya, remember the switch." Helpful reminders can often make all the difference.

4 Children don't have to be happy all the time. Normal everyday disturbances and crises will come and go and are as natural as the sun rising and setting. Eliminating negatives is not about saving our child from every emotional difficulty; rather it is about teaching them methods to use when appropriate. If the truth be told, sometimes a good vent is the best for everyone. Often it clears the air and provides the impetus for change.

5 Establishing healthy emotional habits early in our children's lives ensures that they will choose positive emotions more often than not. Affirmations, visualizing goals, and acknowledging good qualities about themselves are all techniques that enable children to generate attitudes of hope and confidence. An attitude of positive expectancy and a healthy self-image are surefire ways of keeping negatives to a minimum.

7

NO PROBLEMS...
ONLY OPPORTUNITIES

No Problems ...
Only Opportunities

Young children have a unique and powerful capacity to accept whatever "truths" we present to them with conviction and assurance. Since the first ten years of our children's lives form the foundation of their personalities, this is the time to teach them empowering principles that will serve them well on life's journey.

Children should be taught to approach life's challenges with confidence and courage. Temporary failures and setbacks need not discourage them if they have positive beliefs about themselves, and the skills to improvise.

One belief that we encourage children to adopt in our Mind Power for Children program is, "There are no such things as problems; there are only opportunities." Is it true? Well, here's the paradox: it is if you believe it. It's a lot like the old question: Is the glass half full or half empty? Again, it all depends on how you choose to view it. Both views are equally valid and real. From a mind power perspective, we would always choose to see the glass as half full. Why? Firstly, because we can, and secondly, because it positively affects how we feel and think.

The truth is that our perspective on everything is profoundly influenced by the core beliefs we hold. These beliefs form the lens through which we view our world. As conscious parents we recognize the importance of giving our children positive beliefs. Beliefs that make our children more loving, creative and positive are beneficial and empower them. For as we believe, so will we act, and as we act, so do we shape our reality.

In the Mind Power for Children program, we have found that children thrive (adults, too) when they learn to adopt the belief that

EVERY PROBLEM HAS A SOLUTION.

A pessimist sees the difficulty in every opportunity; an optimist sees the opportunity in every difficulty.

» Winston Churchill

there are no such things as problems, only opportunities! Children love to know that for every problem they encounter, there is a solution. In fact, we teach that many solutions exist when they use their creative minds. We impress upon each child the value of being proactive and creative, and the fun of searching out solutions where none appear.

Inventor Buckminster Fuller was a master problem solver. He shares a story about a profound experience that happened to him when he was just four years old. He received his first pair of eyeglasses. Up until then the world seemed fuzzy and out of focus, but when he put on his new glasses everything came into a crystal clear view. From that point on until his death in his eighties, he credited this experience for his tenacity in coming up with innovative solutions for "unsolvable" problems. "I learned at the age of four that if a problem seems difficult and there doesn't seem to be an answer, with persistence you will eventually see it clearly." A powerful belief to learn at four years of age!

We, as parents, can instill in our children the same belief. They deserve to know that whatever problems they are experiencing, there are solutions in abundance. Every problem has a solution and opportunity within it. As the familiar adage says, "Every dark cloud has a silver lining."

Fool on the Hill

The following parable comes from my book *The Practice of Happiness.* We regularly read it to children in our program, and they love to hear the twists and turns of the plot:

A hermit lived on the edge of the forest close to a small village. The villagers all thought he was a fool, for he spoke in paradoxes. His name was Jed. One day Jed took in a stranger who was sick and nursed him back to health. In gratitude the stranger gave him a horse. When the villagers heard what happened they congratulated Jed.

"Jed, what good luck! What great fortune!"

"Who knows if it's good luck?" Jed responded. "Maybe it's bad luck."

"Bad luck?" they laughed. "How can it possibly be that? You had no horse; now you have one. "This is good luck. What a fool!" they thought, "he cannot even recognize good luck when it happens to him."

Jed took his meager savings and bought a saddle. Then one day, the horse escaped and ran away.

mindpower

"Oh, what bad luck," the villagers said when they learned what had happened. "You now have a saddle and no horse."

"Who knows if it's bad luck. Maybe it's good luck," Jed responded cheerfully.

"Good luck?" They laughed. "There's no way this is good luck. This is a tragedy for you."

"Who knows?" said Jed.

Several days later the horse mysteriously returned and brought with him a couple of wild horses. Jed quickly led them into a corral, and word soon spread that he now had three horses. The villagers rushed to see for themselves.

"What good luck!" they said to Jed. "You now have three horses. You can sell two and keep one for yourself."

"Who knows if it's good luck," Jed said. "Maybe it's bad luck that this has happened."

"Bad luck?" they laughed, unable to hide their pity for such a simple-minded fool.

One day while attempting to ride one of the wild horses Jed was thrown and broke his leg.

"What bad luck," the villagers said when they learned of the mishap.

"Who knows," said Jed. "Maybe it's good luck that I broke my leg."

"Good luck?" they all roared with laughter. "You broke your leg. This is obviously a misfortune."

A week later an invading army stormed through the village and forcibly conscripted all the men who were in good health, but they did not take Jed because he had a broken leg.

This parable goes on and on and clearly illustrates to children that no matter what situation they are experiencing, it often changes and reverses itself in the most unexpected ways. This is an important lesson to know when things aren't going the way we want them to.

The Fortunately / Unfortunately Game

This is a favorite storytelling game that works with fantasy problems and positive solution-finding skills. It can be tremendously fun for adults and children of all ages. Begin with either the adult or child introducing a story:

> Once upon a time a family was going for a hike
> in the woods. Unfortunately ... it began to rain.
> Fortunately ... the youngest daughter remembered her umbrella.
> Unfortunately ... the umbrella was broken and the rain could
> come through.

Fortunately ... the girl's brother knew how to
fix umbrellas.
Unfortunately ... he left his tools at home.
Fortunately ... and so on.

Take turns with your children in creating different fantasy "problems" and being the solution finder. The whole family can get into the act. This game is a big hit on those long car rides.

Encourage your child to search independently for answers and solutions when there seem to be none. Don't be so quick to be the solution finder in your house. Whenever someone in your family can't see any way of solving a problem, you can be assured that their thinking is too narrow and restricted. "Be creative, get your mind powers working for you, and let the solutions appear," is a helpful reminder for all of us in these situations.

Practice the "many solutions" technique.

A few good affirmations are:

> *"I always make the right decision."*
> *"Lots of solutions exist."*
> *"I'm smart and creative."*
> *"Every problem has an answer."*

A few moments of affirmations a day can make a huge difference to a child's attitude.

Children are much more capable than we typically believe. Once a child has entered the preschool years, complete dependency upon adults is unhealthy for both parent and child, and counterproductive to the child's further development. Children may try to feign dependency at times, as an excuse to have others do things for them. They may well see certain advantages in pretending to be less capable than they are. However, it is nature's design for children to assert their own independence. If you give children responsibility, they will almost always respond well.

Tomek's family was looking forward to a summer vacation in Montreal. A family reunion had been planned where all of his aunts, uncles and cousins would be together. The only problem was, Tomek had just been given a new puppy dog who was too young to travel by airplane and besides, some of his cousins had allergies to dogs! "I don't know what to do, Mom," he complained. His mother, rather than solve the problem for him, suggested that before dinner he list as many solutions as he could possibly think of on a piece of paper. He should be creative and not even worry about how possible they were. Tomek came up with many imaginative ideas, including putting his puppy in a kennel, hiring a "puppy-sitter," and lending his new puppy to a friend who really liked dogs.

At dinner the family discussed the options and together with Tomek decided that the best solution was to leave the puppy with his friend, George. Tomek was so relieved when George's parents said yes. He also felt very pleased with his solution-finding skills!

PUPPY HOTEL

Risk Taking

Children should be allowed to take risks, unless, of course, they are life threatening. They should be allowed to make mistakes too, since this is how most learning takes place. Resist the urge to save your children from difficult situations that they are able to handle themselves. This doesn't mean, of course, that they will always make

mindPower

wise choices and decisions we agree with. But this is also part of learning. As loving parents, we must also allow our children to make poor choices, since this is how they will learn to make good ones.

> *Believing in our children and enabling them to find their own answers are two of the greatest gifts we can give them.*
> ›› Laura Davis and Janis Keyser

"If you want your kids to make wise choices, give them the opportunity to make lots of choices – including some unwise ones."
›› Barbara Coloroso

Making Mistakes

Making mistakes is a part of life. In fact "getting it wrong sometimes" (a better phrase then "failure") is a normal part of creativity. We often need to remind both ourselves and our children of this important lesson. Only after children learn to separate a person's behavior from the person himself can they begin to tolerate the mistakes of others and themselves.

Author John Maxwell in his book *Failing Foreward* stresses that the difference between those who are successful in life, as opposed to those who are not, relates directly to how they deal with failure at an early age. "Failure," he suggests, "should always be looked at as something temporary, a stepping stone to any eventual success."

He further challenges, "If you could remove the concept of failure from your consciousness, what would you then attempt?" This is a profound question, one that quickly leads to a vastly expanded horizon.

In the process of rebounding from setbacks, children can be reminded of their strengths and be encouraged that "getting it wrong sometimes" has helped many famous people become very successful. After all, Thomas Edison "got it wrong" over ten thousand times when he was inventing the light bulb. Ten thousand times! How is that for persistence? He never thought of himself as a failure. In fact, he once retorted to a well-meaning friend who was offering him consolation, "Why, I have not failed. I've just found ten thousand ways that won't work." Try sharing some of your own experiences of getting it wrong before getting it *right.*

Teaching our children to be proficient at problem solving and coming up with innovative solutions begins by reinforcing that behavior. It's natural and easy to praise children when they are successful. But if they make honest mistakes, be sure to acknowledge your child's resolve to explore new solutions to their problems. This in itself is an important accomplishment for your child. As we discussed in the chapter on acknowledging, future successes are built upon the successes of today. We want to praise the efforts of our children, not just the outcomes.

"You really worked hard on that soccer field today, Brendan. Even though you didn't win this time, you must be pleased with your performance."

"Maggie, I'm so impressed by how patiently you worked on your clay sculpture this afternoon after it fell apart. Your perseverance was an inspiration to the rest of the class."

No problem or temporary difficulty should ever stand in the way of your child's ability to creatively come up with solutions and answers. Let's remember, it is through solving problems that our creative imagination can be exercised. Transforming every problem into an opportunity can become a habit. Our children's confidence soars with the realization that they can rise to every challenge. We, as mind power parents, can help them believe this. Teaching and reinforcing this belief will assist our children to become outstanding solution finders.

Tips for Problem Solving

1 The beliefs our children form about themselves and their capabilities are those we encourage them to practice, and those we model for them with our daily actions. Turning problems into opportunities is a powerful habit and is reinforced through practice.

2 Resist the temptation to come up with solutions and answers to your child's problems. Let them exercise their own problem-solving skills. Often you will be surprised with their innovative approaches. You can always step in as a last resort, but ninety percent of the time your children will work it out for themselves and be the better for it.

mindPower

130

3

MIND POWER

Every time your child solves a personal problem, acknowledge her for her ability. The more you praise children's "problem-solving" skills, the more they will go on to practice this behavior.

4

If the perfect solution existed, what would it look like? Sometimes working backwards from this point allows your child to see the paths necessary to achieve it.

5

"Sleep on it." The subconscious mind works twenty-four hours a day and has access to information we're not consciously aware of. Encourage your child to go to bed and affirm to himself, "My mind will bring me the answer tonight while I sleep." It's truly amazing how answers to problems often come when we let go of them for a while.

MIND POWER

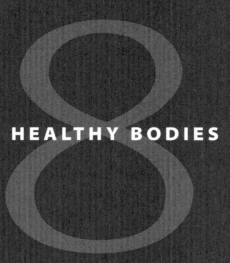

HEALTHY BODIES

Healthy Bodies

Every parent wants his child to be healthy, as opposed to a child who seems to bring home every illness that makes its way through the schoolyard. Fortunately mind power helps us to achieve this goal. Teaching our children to appreciate their bodies' natural ability to maintain vigorous health, combined with the regular practice of mind power techniques, allows our children to take on beliefs that promote health. They begin thinking of themselves as healthy, which is the first step in creating a health consciousness.

Acknowledging the Body

Our bodies are incredible healing mechanisms, designed to maintain maximum health or conquer illness whenever it happens. Sometimes we forget this. For example, when your child cuts himself, healing blood cells immediately rush to the cut. Some of them go to fight any possible infection; others go to congeal the blood. It happens automatically. Our bodies are so efficient and miraculous; they know exactly how to repair themselves. Cuts and scrapes always heal. Always. It's like magic. Colds, measles, mumps, broken arms, toothaches, sprained ankles, the list goes on indefinitely, reaffirming how the body maintains our health. We can use these examples as opportunities to teach our children how strong and healthy their bodies are.

"Mommy I cut myself."

"Here, let's put a bandage on it."

"It hurts."

"I know it does, Sweetheart, but you know what, your body is so healthy and strong that it will completely heal the cut."

"Are you sure?"

"You watch. It will."

As conscious parents we want our children to appreciate their bodies and have healthy beliefs, so helping our child observe and celebrate how marvelous her body is, rather than simply offering

IT'S HEALED!
JUST LIKE
MOM SAID.

sympathy, is excellent imprinting. A couple of days later, when the bandage comes off, you can remark again how the body has healed the cut. How magically the healing process happens. No machines or drugs can do what our bodies do all by themselves.

Every time there is an accident or minor illness, you can use it as an opportunity to reassure your child, "Good thing your body heals itself quickly." And it always does. The body knows how to naturally heal itself. We would be foolish to let this miracle of healing go unnoticed or unappreciated. Always praise and acknowledge your child's ability to naturally recover from illness or injury. Consistency is the key. After a while your child will naturally assume that he can cure himself of anything, and quickly too. After all he's seen it happen countless times – why would he doubt it?

Even in illness, we can praise and acknowledge the healing ability of our bodies. Point out to your child when the occasional sickness does come, that it is the body repairing itself. A cold is the body working extra hard clearing out infections and eliminating mucous so you can be healthy again. If it didn't do that you'd have real problems. The flu activates our immune system and white blood cells rush out to gobble up any viruses. We are so fortunate to have a body that will assist us in such a way. Even in illness, we can praise and acknowledge the healing ability of our bodies.

Health Consciousness

Remember how fascinated you were the first time you saw how wilted plants perk up when they're watered? We do the same thing when we think positive thoughts and acknowledge our body. Consistent healthy

> **The mind is the great healer.**
>
> Hippocrates (the father of medicine)

thoughts are like watering a plant. It makes our body healthy. So too with praising the body. Your child should be taught that a powerful health tonic is her own thoughts. Let's teach our children that having joyful, positive thoughts will do wonders for their disposition and overall state of well-being.

Encourage your children to think, feel and act healthy. Look for opportunities to remind them about what a healthy, strong body they have. Just as a house is built brick by brick, a health consciousness is created thought by thought. This too is an analogy we can share with our children.

Every time your child urinates or has a bowel movement, it is the body discarding waste and impurities. Let her know this is keeping her strong and healthy. We eliminate a number of times each day, and each time is an affirmation of how healthy we are. Every time we eat nutritious food it makes us healthy. Every time we breathe oxygen it makes us healthy. Every time we're outside it makes us healthy. Every time we run and jump it makes us healthy. Every time we think positive thoughts it makes us healthy. Every time we sleep and rest it makes us healthy. We generate health hundreds of times every day. With all this daily positive activity, why wouldn't we be healthy? You and your child can appreciate and acknowledge these health-enhancing activities often.

Children will easily pick up on our expectations, even without our vocalizing them. Children are much more intuitive and aware than we are in this way. Nothing is more powerful in attracting sickness to a child than a parent's fear of it happening. And, heaven forbid, if the parent vocalizes it – "Make sure you don't get sick," or, "Please don't catch a cold." – the emphasis then becomes sickness rather than health. A good mind power maxim to remember is: *what you focus on you attract.*

A good friend of ours recently called in a panic, "They're falling like flies!" she blurted into the telephone. A flu bug was making the rounds at school and she was petrified that her young son would catch it. Instead of affirming to her son how healthy he was, she admonished him, "Please don't get sick – be careful – don't share water bottles – don't touch anyone." Her anxiety was, of course, passed on to her son and both of them began thinking "flu" thoughts. Predictably, he caught the flu and was out of school for almost a week. "Well, he probably would have caught the flu anyway" you might say, but not necessarily. Children who have developed a health consciousness and regularly think healthy thoughts catch far fewer colds, flus and other illnesses then those who don't. This is a fact. A copious amount of research has been done on the positive effects on health of techniques

> *The most beautiful sight in the world is a child walking confidently down the road of life after you have shown him the way.*
>
> ›› Confucius

such as affirmations and visualization, not to mention prayer, which is another form of positive energy. Children who are taught mind power techniques feel inspired to help themselves. One of the great payoffs of health consciousness is self-empowerment.

Ari had come home early from school not feeling well. His brother and sister had a bad gastric bug and had spent the last few days vomiting and feeling feverish. Ari thought he might be coming down with this bug as well. Then he remembered one of the visualizations he had learned at the Mind Power for Children program. It was the healing visualization of imagining healing energy above your head and pulling it down through your body and into the center of the earth, cleansing your body and energizing it.

Ari did the visualization right away, focusing on it for ten minutes. Later that evening he did it again. His mother was amazed at his concentration and determination. Ari never did get the bug, and realized the power of his thoughts to keep his body healthy. He was the only one in the family who didn't get sick!

Healing with your

Visualization for Health

Help your child to get comfortable either lying down or sitting with a straight spine. Ask them to breathe normally with their eyes open or closed, while you read the following healing visualization to them:

"Imagine that just above your head is a ball of white light, like a little white sun. It is full of energy. Breathe in and imagine pulling some of this white light in through the top of your head, into every cell in your body. Breathe out slowly. Breathe in again and feel this light bringing energy into every cell.

Now breathe out and send this light down through your body, out your feet, and way down into the center of the earth. Breathe in again, and pull in some more white light from the ball above your head into every cell of your body.

Breathe the light out, and along with it anything your body no longer needs.

imagination . . .

Breathe in and feel the light bringing you new energy and cleaning every cell in your body. Now breathe out and send the energy down out of your body, through your feet and way into the center of the earth. You are standing under a waterfall of light. It's like a magic shower giving you energy and washing you clean. You feel radiantly healthy. You look radiantly healthy too.

*Now breathe in and bring the white light into any part of your body that could use some healing. This energizes the cells to heal more quickly. Breathe out any pain or discomfort. Breathe in the good energy again. Now breathe out, sending the discomfort through your feet way down into the center of the earth. Your whole body feels energetic and brimming with health. Now, finish by putting a picture of yourself up on your movie screen and seeing your whole body as **fit, strong,** and **healthy**.*

Well done. Open your eyes. Good visualizing!"

There are many different visualizations you can teach your children regarding health. One is a general visualization of seeing and feeling themselves in perfect health. This can include breathing in health with every breath, imagining their blood circulating and purifying their body, feeling the strength of their arms and legs, etc. Even a two- or three-minute guided visualization can help focus your child's thoughts on health.

There is no hard and fast rule as to what to visualize or affirm. Let your imagination guide you. The point to remember is that we are encouraging our child to think of herself as healthy – she will naturally gravitate towards her own favorite ways of imagining health once the concept is introduced and practiced.

Let Their Bodies Speak to Them

"If your sore leg could talk ... what would it tell us?"

Teaching our children to listen to their body is the most effective way to open communication between their minds and bodies. The notion of creating a dialogue with a sore leg might seem a bit weird to us as adults; to a child, though, it will probably resonate as a very natural thing to do. Intuitive work must always be approached with sincerity, regardless of how foreign or new it may seem. Children can pick up on whether *"Mommy thinks this is going to work,"* or *"Mommy has her doubts about this."*

When your child listens to his body and asks questions like, *"What do you want me to know about you?"* you'll be amazed at what might come out.

"My legs are so sore it's like their crying," moaned Terry.
"Gee, Terry, what do you think they're trying to tell you?" asked Mom.
"They're saying, 'We want a rest … we want a rest,'" replied Terry.
Mom laughed and said, "Well, even the very strongest athletes need to give their legs a rest after three hours of soccer practice and an afternoon of skating."

Mom was right and so was Terry. Another time, Mom might have become unnecessarily alarmed and added to the pain rather than the cure. Most aches and pains are so transitory that the less we make of them the quicker they go away. Of course, when problems persist it's important to have them checked by a physician. The majority of doctors, however, report that most of their patients could do with more *patience*. And doctors experience daily how efficient and miraculous our bodies are. Let us trust our bodies to heal us as they were designed to do.

When my cousin Janet broke her arm at age four, she was really worried. In fact she was inconsolable as she lay crying in her hospital bed. The last "broken" arm she had seen, belonged to her china doll.

She thought that her arm was filled with broken pieces that could never be repaired! Once she realized the truth, she relaxed. Her mom helped her to imagine her arm strong and healthy again – they visualized the bone healing in exactly the way her scratches had healed. They even talked to the arm, telling it what a strong and healthy arm it was. It healed perfectly. » Kim

The more your children know, trust and love their bodies, the happier and healthier they will be.

Healing With Affirmations

Affirm to your child, "You're really healthy." Let him appreciate and acknowledge his own health. Become health conscious yourself. You can practice together the affirmation, "I'm really healthy."

These sorts of affirmations can be said daily. They can also be printed on an acknowledging poster for your child to see every day, further imprinting the concept. Signs and daily affirmations act as a miracle tonic, combating the first sign of a cold or flu.

Valerie, age seven, came home the other day sniffling and announced, "Mom I'm getting a cold."

"No you're not dear," I countered. "You've just got a few sniffles. You're so healthy and strong that your body will naturally fight off the cold."

(144)

mindpower

"Yeah?" she responded, not entirely convinced.

"You watch," I said confidently. "In fact, I'm going to take you out to a movie tomorrow to celebrate your good health."

"Really ... in the middle of the week?"

A midweek movie is not normal for our family, but I wanted to encourage her to be healthy. We did a few minutes of affirming, "I'm really healthy," together, and Valerie, with the thought of the movie in her mind, did it enthusiastically.

HEALTH DAY AT THE MOVIES

That night I heard her use the "I'm really healthy" affirmation without any prompting. She did it in the morning too, as soon as she was awake.

As promised we went to the movies, Valerie without so much as a sniffle. That experience taught us both the power of affirmations. » Lynn, a Mind Power parent

"Every day in every way I'm getting better and better."
This popular affirmation is a favorite of children. It's simple yet so powerful and effective. They love saying it to themselves. One mind power student used this affirmation to heal his wart:

My son Charles, when he was six, had been to the doctor for a very painful plantar's wart, deeply rooted in the sole of his foot. He was booked to have treatment for its removal a week later, but when the day arrived, Charles told me that the wart was almost completely gone. Upon checking, I saw that it was true and called the doctor to cancel the appointment. When I asked Charles what he had done, he told me that he had looked at his foot every day and said, "My foot is getting better and better every day!" Both his father and I were thrilled. Not only that he had healed his foot, but that he had used the mind power technique on his own without any prompting. Sometimes children have more faith than we do! » Simone

Never underestimate the power of words and visual images to assist the body in maintaining health and healing all common ailments. Mind power techniques offer simple and powerful preventative maintenance to keep our children healthy and illness free.

> *Children are apt to*
> *live up to what you*
> *believe of them.*
> » Lady Bird Johnson

Tips
to Promote Health Consciousness

mindPower

148

1 Look for opportunities to celebrate your children's good health. Encourage them to think of themselves as healthy and strong. Guide them in adopting healthy beliefs.

2 MIND POWER

Minimize the attention your child receives for illnesses and accidents when they occur. Too often bandages on cuts and plaster casts on broken limbs become the focus of attention. Sick or injured children are often given prestige because of their situation. Unlimited TV, extra attention and special treats are some of the ways we unintentionally encourage sickness. This is far from healthy in any genuine sense of the word. Remembering that behavior which is rewarded is repeated; we need to find ways to express our sympathy without glamorizing an unwelcome condition.

3 Reward good health just as you would positive behavior. One parent we know gives her child a "health" day off from school every couple of months. Her son gets the day off "for being so healthy," and they do fun things together. The message is that he doesn't have to be sick to get a day off school.

4 Hold the vision of perfect health for your children. Dare to believe, along with them, that they will be incredibly healthy. Watch that fear or "common sense" doesn't seduce you into believing that infirmity has greater power over your children than their belief in health. Your child has more control over his health than you might think.

5 Encourage your children to use health affirmations regularly and to see themselves as healthy. Visualize and acknowledge excellent health daily. A day-by-day dose of healthy thoughts and expectations is a wonderful health tonic. Each day can begin with an, "I'm really healthy," or an, "Every day in every way I'm getting better and better" affirmation. Health consciousness is maintained through regular application of the mind power techniques.

MIND POWER

9

MAKING FRIENDS

Making Friends

Making new friends is an important part of growing up. Whether our children are switching schools, moving to another city or just going through changes, they often find themselves seeking out new friends.

It seems to go in cycles. Sometimes there are lots of friends around, and other times it appears that no one likes us. Making new friends can sometimes seem like a daunting task to a little one. As parents, we can assist our children by reminding them of their positive qualities and by offering helpful advice on how to make friends.

WHEN I GROW UP I'M GONNA HAVE LOTS OF FRIENDS JUST LIKE MOM.

Modeling Friendship

Children learn their first lessons about making friends from observing us. Demonstrate the qualities and effort necessary to make new friends and keep old friendships going. Let them see what is required to have quality friendships. Your children will learn a lot from your good example.

"Sorry, Carey, I would be happy to go shopping for running shoes with you after school today, but my friend Susan is counting on me to help her paint her back porch. Can we make a plan for tomorrow instead? That way we can still have fun together and I won't have to disappoint my friend."

While your child may be disappointed that you won't go shopping with her, she will have learned a significant lesson about the importance of honoring friendship. With your positive model to follow, your children will naturally begin to develop the attributes of a loyal friend.

Acknowledging

Everyone likes to be acknowledged for the positive qualities they possess. As your child demonstrates the characteristics of a true friend, choose appropriate moments to acknowledge these positive characteristics in them.

"I really like the way you included Brendan in your game today, John."

"I know why other children like playing with you, Stephanie. You always share your toys and know how to take turns."

Take any opportunity that presents itself to notice and acknowledge friendship qualities in your child and the other people around them. Genuine compliments will certainly serve to reinforce that behavior.

Reinforcing That Your Child Is Likable

Your acknowledgements will also strengthen in your child the idea that she is likable. Children who like themselves, and are convinced that others like them, make friends easily.

Make an Acknowledging list and post it on your child's bedroom wall, the refrigerator, or anywhere that it can be read often.

WHY I'M A GREAT PERSON TO HAVE AS A FRIEND:

> I'm kind.
> I'm generous.
> I know how to have fun.
> I know how to take turns.
> I share my toys.
> I like playing games.

This list will act as a reminder of all your children's good qualities, and reinforce their belief in themselves. Your children will probably want to contribute ideas themselves once you have started. You could also make a list of all the qualities *they* would like in a new friend.

Once you have this second list, you could ask your child if she is doing these things herself, because other people might be looking for the same qualities in a friend. You are taking the first steps towards teaching your child that the sort of person she is has a direct bearing on the number of friends she will attract.

Be the Person You'd Like As a Friend

An optimistic child radiates positive energy and attracts people.

Nobody likes to be with a sullen, moody person. It's wise to remember that what we project into the world, we usually receive back. Helping your child to feel happy, loved and special will in itself always act as a magnet for friends.

Affirmations

"I make friends easily."
"People like me."
"I'm a great friend to have."

These and numerous other positive affirmations are a wonderful way to start the day. Repeating them ten times before heading off to school in the morning sets the tone for a terrific day and sends your children off with a positive attitude about themselves.

In a previous chapter we advised that bedtime is a good time to suggest positive ideas because your child's mind is so receptive at that point. Here is an idea to try after their bedtime. Before you go to bed, gently whisper some positive statements into your child's ear while he is sleeping. *"Everybody likes you. You are good at making friends."* It's worth doing, as your child's subconscious is wide open to beneficial suggestions while he is asleep.

As a complement to these positive messages, add a note to their lunchbox. We have witnessed numerous times the delightful response of children who discover an encouraging lunchbox note from someone who loves them. It's a perfect time to acknowledge your children for the wonderful people they are, and remind them of the positive friendship qualities they possess. When these notes get shared with curious friends, it further serves to implant the positive ideas in their mind.

Visualization for New Friends

When your child is on a low cycle of friendship, it may seem to him like he'll never ever have another good friend again. We, of course, know better, but children don't have our life experience. It's easy for them to fall into negative thinking, imagining that it'll just never ever happen.

If your child finds herself in a spell of gloom, thinking about the lack of friends, a guided visualization can really help out. A daily five-minute session of seeing herself at school, on the playground, at the swimming pool, meeting new friends and getting along well with them, will do wonders. Not only will it make your child feel happier and build up her confidence, but it creates positive expectations as well. The first few times it may seem like she's just fooling herself, but we've never known a child to do this visualization for two weeks without meeting a new friend. It works like magic.

If your child has recently experienced a negative encounter with another child, you might talk about how it might have been different; what could have happened to create a happier outcome to the situation. After this discussion, a visualization of this positive outcome will replace the negative images and feelings, and provide your child with empowering images to carry with him, along with positive expectations of future experiences.

Responding to a Negative Attitude

"Nobody likes me, everybody hates me - I'm going down the garden to eat some worms." ›› Anonymous

Nothing warms our heart like knowing our children have friends. We want so much for our children to relate well to others and be liked. The time will come, however, when she comes home and announces, "Nobody wants to play with me," or, "Everybody hates me." Your first reaction may be sudden worry, but try not to panic. Your child will pick up on the importance you attach to these words, so you need to respond carefully. You may find yourself wanting to deny such a situation by saying, "I can't believe that's true. Everyone likes you." Such a direct contradiction may only serve to invite resistance: "No they don't. Nobody likes me." A more effective way is to listen carefully, reminding your child of her positive qualities.

Then, rather than making too much of the complaint, which only gives energy to a negative situation, suggest some solutions, or better yet, encourage her to do so. You might say, "If there was another little girl in a different city exactly your age in the exact same situation, what suggestions would you give to her for making friends?" This is sure to spark some insights into her own situation. Offer gentle reminders of past occasions when your child made friends, or where people showed how much they enjoyed your child's company.

"Remember when you met that new boy Brent at the park and he invited you to play soccer with him? Do you want to invite Emily over to play later?"

This is an excellent chance to casually introduce some of the mind power techniques to counter any further episodes. Be casual. Your child may pick up on your suggestion or she may not, this time. All you need to do initially is to supply a positive alternative to your child's negative message. You and she can build on it later. The thing to remember when your child is in a friendship drought is that, with children, it is *always* temporary.

Remember, however, that when you help your child find ways to deal with difficult friendship issues, it's important that those problems don't become *your* problems. Our role as parents is not to be our daughter or son's best friend. Resist, for example, the urge to join your child at school for lunch, just so he has someone to sit with. These temporary "solutions" will only prolong the problem.

Let Them Talk to Strangers – A Contrarian View

During the course of our lives, most of the people we meet and have connections with are *strangers*. Our childhood friends were once *strangers*. The people we spent time with in high school were once *strangers*, and the people we work with were once *strangers*. Your husband or wife was once a *stranger*. Instead of teaching our children to fear and avoid strangers, let's teach them how to respond to strangers in an appropriate way, and allow our children the chance to develop better interpersonal skills.

When it comes right down to it, there are a great many strangers

> *Children who are given the opportunity to help others tend to become more helpful in their everyday lives. This is especially true if the effect of their kind actions on the people they helped was specifically pointed out to them.*
> ›› Dr. Ervin Staub, University of Massachusetts

in the world. If we tell our children not to talk to any of them, whom *are* they going to talk to? And in saying this, what message are we giving to our children?

   We can secure our children's physical safety without damaging their emotional security. We do it by focusing on the positive. Let them talk to strangers. Just tell them not to go anywhere with them. Why? Because you, their parent, have to know where your children are at all times. You will find that your children will be only too happy to comply with such a reasonable request. This way you needn't damage their faith in others. You never know when your child might be dependent on a stranger for his well-being one day.

   I remember an occasion two years ago when I was in the changing rooms at the swimming pool preparing for a swim. I noticed a child, about age nine, searching around the rooms and appearing more and more distraught. She was alone and seemed to be looking for someone or something. After several minutes she sat down on a bench near me and started crying. I went over and asked her what was wrong. I reached out to touch her shoulder and she quickly pulled back from me, crying even harder. I said, "If you tell me what's wrong I might be able to help." In a voice of total despair she said through her tears, "I'm not allowed to talk to strangers."

My heart went out to her. I sat down beside her and said that I had a daughter who was about her age, so it would probably be all right to talk to me. "I'm lost," she wailed. "I can't find the door out to the pool." (It was around the corner behind a wall and, to the uninitiated, not easy to find.) More sobs. I said, "I'll show you. Come with me." I intended taking her to her mother; she was that upset.

When we reached the entrance to the pool, she turned to me and said, "I'll be all right now." I suggested that I stay with her until we found her mother. "Don't come," she pleaded, crying again. "If Mom sees me talking to a stranger I'll get in big trouble." Against my better judgment I let her go alone. She was in such a terrible state I didn't want to add to it. This child was surrounded by helpful strangers, but was unable to ask for help because she had been conditioned to distrust strangers. » Carla

It's time to step outside the fear consciousness that pervades our society. Instead of teaching our children to run from an encounter, let's teach them how to handle a variety of situations. In your child's hour of need, a "stranger" is a thousand times more likely to be a friend than someone who would hurt him. If we teach our children to always suspect the kindness of others, we are cutting them off from guidance, countless nourishing experiences and

If I could design the ideal environment for educating students, it would be based upon the philosophy that relationships are primary.

>> Sherleen Sisney, 1984 National Teacher of the Year

potential help when it might be needed. No one is going to climb a mountain if they have been inculcated with the fear of falling, just as no one is going to develop consistent healthy relationships with others if they have been taught to fear and distrust all strangers. Teach your children trust and boundaries, not fear and isolation. Teach them how to handle chance encounters. Allow them to talk to strangers in appropriate situations. Make a point of doing it yourself to show them how.

Tips

for Making Friends (And Keeping the Ones You Have!)

1

Plan to include a new friend in an upcoming event – going bowling, to a movie, making cookies, etc. When considering a new extracurricular activity for your children, such as a sports team, piano lessons or dance, you might want to invite a new friend along to join in the fun. Chances are good that another child will be keen on the activity, and his parents will appreciate an opportunity to carpool.

2

Children can learn to give appreciation to friends by sending a thank-you note after a party, or a "thinking of you" card. Friendships need nurturing too, and it makes everyone feel better.

mindPower

164

F O R

C H I L D R E N

3

MIND POWER

Invite another parent from your child's class over for coffee so that your child has a friend to play with as a result of your activity. Make it low key. "Elizabeth's Mom is coming for a visit after school on Tuesday and Elizabeth is coming too," is better than saying, "I've arranged for Elizabeth to come over on Tuesday so you can make friends." If your child is resistant, you needn't worry or change your plans. In creating friendships you have to start somewhere, and in the long run, your child needs to get along with others whether she instantly likes the idea or not. The skills your child develops on these occasions will stand her in good stead for years to come.

4

In arranging such get-togethers, ask your child's teacher to suggest a child with similar interests and disposition. Such a conversation will often also prompt the teacher to support the new friendship at school, say by suggesting that the two children become partners for a Science Fair project.

Tips

for Making Friends (And Keeping the Ones You Have!)

5

Plan a multi-family garage sale or family picnic. Community gatherings of any kind bring children of all ages together. Your children may discover new friends who already live in your neighborhood.

6

Make posters extolling your child's good friendship qualities. Acknowledge that he is doing well. Take advantage of this observation to promote further appropriate behavior in the future.

7

If times are lean, encourage your child to visualize having friends, playing and having fun with them. Situations such as the first day of school, a sleepover at a friend's home, or an upcoming sporting event are also ideal times to help your child use visualization techniques.

mindpower

166

MAKING FRIENDS

10

OUR CHILD'S FUTURE BEGINS TODAY

Our Child's Future Begins Today

There is an African proverb that beautifully summarizes the real-ity of child rearing: "It takes a village to raise a child." The meaning is crystal clear. Children need lots of input. They need parents, grand-parents, aunts, uncles, family friends, strangers and a host of oth-er well-meaning people to give them the necessary experiences and mentoring to become well-adjusted and balanced members of our society.

Up until quite recently this was how children were raised. Every-one lived together or within close proximity to one another. Mom, dad, grandparents, kids, cousins, uncles; the extended family was ever present and available for celebrations, crises, and day-to-day goings-on. In the 21st century, it's radically different. Statistics show that there are now more children being raised by single parents than by couples, and even within the two-parent families, less than twenty percent of them have a stay-at-home mom or dad. More than ever before, parents are feeling over-extended and isolated; more than ever they're seeking support anywhere they can find it. Perhaps it is time to design new strategies to allow our children more love and mentoring from a greater diversity of people. Let's rethink our whole concept of family.

What Is Normal?

What do *normal* families really look like anyway? Well, they look like our families. They come in many different sizes, shapes, styles and colors. Today we see women and men coming together to form family groupings in a whole variety of new and different ways. There are single parents, teenage parents, adoptive parents and same-sex parents. Some children are raised by their grandparents or aunts and uncles. With more than fifty percent of school-age children now living in "nontraditional" families, it's reasonable to conclude that it's time we redefine our concept of what is normal.

The extended family has always been a very integral part of the "village." Family meals, holiday celebrations, birthdays, sleepovers, weekends at the cottage, a night at grandma's, a hockey game with

Uncle Bob, all these activities help to raise our children well. Grandparents, aunts, uncles and cousins all contribute to our children's understanding of how people relate to one another. Children watch carefully to learn about life from people they love and trust. Marriages, childbirth, sickness and even death are significant events that constitute the mixed blessings of family life.

Let's Reinvent the Village

But while immediate family is where we initially look for mentoring and help, we cannot afford to stop there. Too often in our modern, busy and transient lives our family may not even be in the same city. Here we can widen our concepts of who can help our children. We cannot let our reservations about strangers block the immense nurturing and mentoring that can and will happen when we trust in the basic goodness of people. Our children need "the village," and if the old village doesn't exist nowadays, then we are obliged to create a new one.

Whenever I held my newborn baby in my arms, I used to think that what I said and what I did to him could have an influence not only on him but on all whom he met, not only for a day or a month or a year, but for all eternity.

>> Rose Kennedy

These times call for new and creative measures, and it starts with a change of attitude within ourselves. No matter how loving and ever present we are with our children, they still need and deserve more. We can't do it all by ourselves. We were never meant to do it alone.

We Need More Uncle Bobs

"When my oldest child was smaller, we spent a lot of time in the company of an old friend of mine who quickly became known as "Uncle Bob," even though he was in no way related to us by blood. Like many contemporary families we had very few relatives living nearby. Bob lived in a recreational area north of the city, and when we visited him there he would often mind our children while we went skiing. Sometimes he would take us all out for a bike ride, or simply play with the kids in the backyard. Our children loved going to his house, and he enjoyed us visiting. Eventually Bob moved away, but for the three years he lived close by, he was an excellent source of nurturing, fun and adventure for our children." ›› David, father of two

If we're going to re-create a new and modern village for our children, we're going to need a lot more Uncle Bobs. And where are these Uncle Bobs or Aunt Bobbys? They are everywhere, and in greater numbers than you would suspect.

They are the strangers who are in your own neighborhood. Make some of them your acquaintances, as opportunities arise. A request for help from a friend, neighbor, or your community is a sacred opportunity, one to be cherished, and followed up on immediately. Let's reach out to people. Whether it's stopping to help someone push their stalled car, shovel their sidewalk free of snow while you're shoveling yours, or asking if your neighbor, who doesn't drive, would like to travel with you to the supermarket at the edge of town, it's all part of creating the village.

Volunteer some of your time, too. Yes, we know you're busy, but if the truth be told, the best way to find an Uncle Bob is to be one yourself.

*Publisher Rex Weyler did just that when he formed a soccer club for his eight-year-old son. His son was having problems with self-esteem because he was a poor reader. But he was an excellent athlete. Rex understood that when a child enjoys success in one area it often helps in other areas as well. So even though he could not afford the time away from his growing publishing business, he **made** the time. The soccer team excelled and even won their tournament. Rex's son's self-esteem went through the roof and his reading improved remarkably. For all the other boys on the team and their parents, Rex became part of their "village." Not only that, but he found the experience incredibly rewarding and a welcome break from his business.*

174

mindpower

When you take the time to help others, help will come to you, often in the most unexpected ways.

Singer, songwriter and single mother, Ann Mortifee, was having discipline problems with her young son. Nothing dramatic, just the usual frustrations of adolescence. Ann is a very loving and giving individual, always helping friends and strangers alike, and she realized, as a female caregiver, that her son needed something she couldn't give him. She began to imagine a mentor for her son. When you practice mind power and trust in life, remarkable things really do happen. Her son soon heard of a martial arts class being offered in his neighborhood. He joined. Adam, the twenty-year-old instructor, took a liking to Devon and a friendship formed between them. Discipline – military style – was his modus operandi. Devon thrived with the encouragement and attention, while his mother watched his innate nobility emerge in the months that followed.

When Feeling Helpless or Alone, Think "Village"

If we are to rebuild the modern village, we are all called upon to help. Grandparents, aunts and uncles, teachers, friends, everyone has a role to play. It is here we find ourselves looking within. If we are a grandfather (and I hope grandparents are reading this book – if not give them a copy) we ask, "What does that mean, to be a grandfather? What are the possibilities, options, responsibilities?" How can we mentor our grandchildren; what gifts of love, appreciation and learning can we give? What does it mean to be an uncle, an aunt, or a close family friend? If we are to build the village, then we all need to play an active role. Parents can't always do it on their own. Sending a card twice a year is no longer enough. If everyone felt inspired to cultivate a special relationship with a child and acted upon that impulse, the village would be created overnight. What a wonderful dream and vision that is.

As parents, we also need to think "village." We need to believe that beyond the façade of our modern busy life, people are good, loving, and want to help. If we want a "village" then let's have the courage to change our attitudes and begin thinking and acting "village" in our lives. It starts with one person at a time. It starts with us.

Getting Friends and Relatives to Help

A child's life is like a piece of paper on which everyone who passes by leaves an impression.

>> Chinese proverb

One thing that every new parent relies on is support from friends, other parents and relatives. Although everything from breastfeeding to private schools might be subject to debate, the experience of others who care for you and your family will always be your most valuable resource. Since those closest to you will already be a part of your child-rearing team, your "village," why not introduce them to your new mind power for children techniques. The more people who support the empowerment of your children the better. Gradually introduce the notion of *mind power* to the members of your child's extended family. It will be helpful to remember that, as committed as you are to being positive with your children, well-meaning relatives may find your "new" ideas a bit radical at first.

"Auntie Lou, Mom says I don't have to be 'realistic,' says Emily, "I just want to be positive!"

"Really," replies Aunt Lou, turning to Emily's mom, "Are you into some new religion, Joan?"

Even the most open-minded relatives may take some time to acclimatize to your new role as a parent, let alone your new approach to child rearing.

"Chani tells me she's got an 'energy shield' that protects her if the kids at school tease her about her braces. I've never heard of such a thing!"

mindpower

The next step is to give your family an overview of the goals you and your children have, and explain how you are expecting positive results. Maybe even suggest ways in which they can support your child's efforts, thus making them part of the team. Then you can share with them the positive changes that you see in your child's behavior, attitude and self-esteem.

"Guess what, Dad," says Joan, "Emily's been trying some new mind power exercises we've been learning about. Every day she reminds herself that she can be anything she wants and wow, what a difference it has made at school. Emily's confidence has improved so much. She's even trying out for the track team,

OUR FUTURE LEADERS

something she used to think she couldn't do! Isn't that great news?"

Naturally, Dad will be happy to hear this news, and will have had a positive introduction to mind power.

Most importantly, encourage your children to share their mind power success stories with their grandparents, aunts, uncles and friends. After all, even the most stubborn relative can be swept away by enthusiasm.

"Well, Chani," says her grandad, "having an energy shield is a new idea to me, but if it makes wearing braces to school any easier, I'm sure happy you have one."

Teaching our children mind power isn't simply an isolated interaction between parent and child, teacher and student, or uncle and nephew, it is a revolutionary act. Each time we practice it, we are becoming co-creators in an exciting new way of empowering children. Thousands now use this system and before we know it, our children will be passing it on to their own children. This is a powerful movement.

Ultimately, our children belong to the world. Their destiny at birth is to leave us, to venture out into the world as adults and to create their own lives. We hope that, through our guidance, they will have identified their talents, skills and intelligence, and that they will be able to become whatever they choose. We desire for them only happiness, but the world desires for them much more. The world desires that they become the surgeons, scientists, inventors, plumbers, poets, mystics, pharmacists and teachers of the next generation; that their genius, encoded within them at birth, will awaken and bear fruit.

As conscious parents we realize that the foundation of our child's matrix is created under our stewardship. Enthusiasm for life, healthy self-image, a positive attitude, empathy for others, creative solution finding, the ability to rebound from setbacks, all these can be cultivated and nurtured in our children. By parenting our children well in a mind power way, we are adding to the value of the human community. The village is better off for us and our children being here.

It's Up to Each of Us

Now that you're coming to the end of this book, are you ready to embrace this new way of thinking? You're convinced of the power of the mind and you want to make a difference in your child's life, but where do you start? Take one step at a time. With practice, your understanding of the mind's ability to manifest numerous changes in you and your child's life will become second nature. In fact, our children will probably make this shift in thinking faster than we do, since they haven't been conditioned as long as we have in the "old" way of thinking. As parents, we examine what beliefs and values we wish our children to realize, and we work to give them these insights. Our children will benefit from our positive vision of prosperity, self-confidence and generosity. Our diligence will bear fruit.

Mind Power for Children Works!

The tried and true techniques we have described in this book have proven successful for thousands of children, and they will work with yours too! As your children's mind power mentor, you now have the tools to help them grow into positive, productive and successful human beings capable of achieving goals that you may only have dreamed of when you were their age.

Each generation evolves both intellectually and spiritually from the values and beliefs they have inherited from the generation preceding them. Today is the womb through which the future will emerge. We sow seeds for our children's tomorrow by our actions today. In the grand scheme of the universe unfolding, no act goes without consequence. Everything we do makes a difference when we parent in a conscious way. The ripple effect of our parenting will expand beyond our own children. It will touch every person they come in contact with. It will impact on their children and their children's children.

We now have more than just hope for our children; we have a system of empowerment. The destiny of the planet lies in the hands of these young people. Each of us, as members of the "global village," has both the honor and obligation to prepare our children for the challenges and responsibilities of adulthood. Let's work together, all of us, to foster a generation of self-assured, clear thinkers, and dare to believe that the world will be changed one child at a time. This is our vision.

Learn More About Mind Power

Visit us at: **www.learnmindpower.com**

As writers committed to staying in touch with their readers, John Kehoe and Nancy Fischer personally invite you to join them via the Internet to share your Mind Power questions and observations. Each month John and Nancy will respond to a selection of correspondence on matters of interest to their ever-expanding community of readers, parents and teachers. You will also find

this exciting website loaded with important news and information updates, topics of the month, questions and answers, tour schedules, interesting links, and tips on using Mind Power. Contact John and Nancy by directing your browser to:

http://www.learnmindpower.com

Good Advice from Kids

"Never trust a dog to watch your food."
» Patrick, age 10

*"When your Dad is mad and asks you,
'Do I look stupid?' Don't answer."*
» Hannah, age 9

"Never tell your Mom her diet's not working."
» Michael, age 14

*"When your Mom is mad at your Dad,
don't let her brush your hair."*
» Taylia, age 11

*"Never let your three-year-old brother
in the same room as your school assignment."*
» Traci, age 10

*"You can't hide a piece of broccoli
in a glass of milk."*
» Amir, age 9

*"If you want a kitten, start out by
asking for a horse."*
» Naomi, age 8

*"Felt-tip markers are not good
to use as lipstick."*
» Lauren, age 9

*"Don't pick on your sister when she's
holding a baseball bat."*
» Joel, age 10

Mind Power Into the 21st Century

In *Mind Power Into the 21st Century*, John Kehoe has articulated a set of life-changing principles for charting a course to success and happiness. More than that, however, *Mind Power Into the 21st Century* presents a remarkably specific and practical guide.

How to:
* harness the powers of your subconscious mind
* tap into your creativity
* successfully use visualization techniques
* improve your self-image
* interpret your dreams
* heal yourself
* develop a "prosperity consciousness"
* build and maintain fulfilling relationships

ISBN 0-9697551-4-7

Also by John Kehoe:

The Practice of Happiness

Money, Success & You

A Vision of Power and Glory

"Presents a remarkably specific and practical guide that shows the reader how to harness the powers of their subconscious mind."

BOOKWATCH

" ...a treasure of important ideas and practical techniques."

DAVID FEINSTEIN,
CO-AUTHOR OF PERSONAL MYTHOLOGY

" This book is for everybody."

METRO NETWORK